THE FIVE
SEASONS

TAP INTO NATURE'S SECRETS FOR

HEALTH, HAPPINESS, AND HARMONY

THE FIVE
SEASONS

JOSEPH CARDILLO, PHD

New Page BOOKS

A division of
The Career Press, Inc.
Pompton Plains, N.J.

THE FIVE SEASONS
EDITED AND TYPESET BY KARA KUMPEL
Cover design by John Moore
Printed in the U.S.A.

To order this title, please call toll-free 1-800-CAREER-1 (NJ and Canada: 201-848-0310) to order using VISA or MasterCard, or for further information on books from Career Press.

The Career Press, Inc.
220 West Parkway, Unit 12
Pompton Plains, NJ 07444
www.careerpress.com
www.newpagebooks.com

Library of Congress Cataloging-in-Publication Data
Cardillo, Joseph.
 The five seasons : tap into nature's secrets for health, happiness, and harmony / by Joseph Cardillo, PhD.
     pages cm
 Includes bibliographical references and index.
 ISBN 978-1-60163-258-6 (print) -- ISBN 978-1-60163-535-8 (ebook)
     1. Happiness. 2. Life cycle, Human. 3. Conduct of life. I. Title.

BF575.H27C3714 2013
158--dc23

                                                              2013007248

For my wife, Elaine, and our daughters, Isabella and Veronica, whom we loved before they were born, and to my father and mother, Alfio and Josephine Cardillo.

ACKNOWLEDGMENTS

I wish to thank my immediate family and extended family for their energies and guidance in helping bring this project to completion. I wish to acknowledge my niece, Anna Cardillo, for her graphics assistance and encouragements.

Special thanks are extended to my wife, Elaine, for her love, friendship, creative and strong mind, and support along this journey; and to our beautiful, inspirational, and talented daughters, Isabella and Veronica, for all their goodness, magnificence, and balance.

Thanks to Matt Papa as well as all my martial arts associates, partners, and colleagues for their support, brotherhood, and sisterhood.

Special thanks to my agent, Linda Konner; to all my publicists; and everyone at Career Press/New Page Books, especially Ron Fry, Michael Pye, Adam Schwartz, Laurie Kelly-Pye, Kirsten Dalley, Jeff Piasky, Allison Olson, Kara Kumpel, and Gina Talucci.

Thanks to Joseph Cavalcante for our many conversations on the craft of writing.

Thanks to Lon Normandin for his encouragement and support.

It is with deep gratitude that I acknowledge my parents, Alfio and Josephine Cardillo, for their gifts of love, encouragement, and life.

DISCLAIMER

The case examples in this book are drawn from media accounts or are composite examples based upon behaviors encountered in the author's own professional experiences. None of the individuals described were patients or clients. The names and details have been changed to protect the privacy of the people involved.

This publication does not claim to be medical advice. It is not intended as a substitute for the advice of healthcare professionals.

Before engaging in any physical, psychological, or spiritual training programs, you should always check with your physicians and other professional healthcare providers to be sure that it is right for you.

One touch of nature makes the whole world kin.
—William Shakespeare

Centuries ago, the Asian philosophers noticed how the rising and falling energies of the seasons influenced the mind, body, and spirit in specific and identifiable ways. They concluded that by tapping into nature's seasonal energy, you could live longer, healthier, and happier.

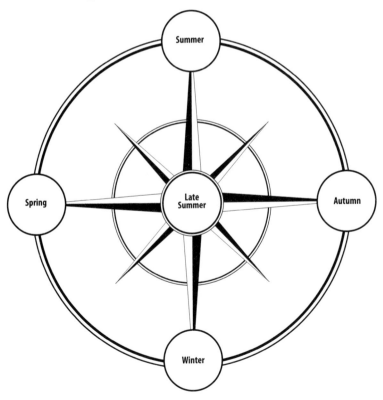

CONTENTS

Winter

INTRODUCTION

The number 5 has a distinct position in Eastern wisdom and especially in Traditional Chinese Medicine (TCM). Its significance is based on the continuous cycle of five *universal movements* (or seasons) and the unique *chi* (energy) generated by each.

In TCM, everything in the universe, from largest to smallest, is influenced by these movements. Collectively, they describe nature's continuous cycle of *rising and falling energy*. Being aware of these cycles and understanding how they work is at the heart of all self-improvement.

Because we are a part of nature and nature is a part of us, these energy movements describe not only the rising and falling of energies in our external environment, but also the *up* and *down* energy you feel minute by minute, event by event, conversation by conversation, thought by thought, throughout your day, week, month, year, and so on. You can feel the effects of this momentum physically and emotionally. When you sync up just right (harmonize) with these cycles, you feel as though you are doing everything with ease. You feel good inside and out, as though all is going the best it can for you.

In a way, these five universal movements operate in our mind-body like a network, running virtually without our awareness—most of the time. With a little information you can, however, become much more aware of them and their abundant influence. You can then begin using these rhythms to strategically influence and improve your life. The trick is learning how to sync up and stay connected.

Becoming aware of the special components of each energy cycle and how they contribute to keeping you healthy, happy, and harmonious, from within and without, is the first step. At its best, this kind of awareness also helps you use nature's energies to bring out the most in others. Ultimately, if you change the way you understand and use nature's energy you will change your life and contribute the best of you to everyone you touch.

According to TCM, there are five types of energy (chi) in nature that dominate at different times within the seasonal (and all smaller, including minute-by-minute) cycles. You're probably wondering, similar to so many of the people I have spoken to on this topic, what the fifth season is.

The additional season is what we in the West refer to as late (or Indian) summer, a time when the earth's productive cycle reaches its peak and which is followed by a time of declining energy and energy storage. Late summer is the middle season. The world of holistic arts and sciences places much importance on this concept of *middle* or *center*. Indeed, the word *China* itself translates to "middle country."

Indian summer, the fifth season, is energetically important because it provides the *hub* or *center of balance* for the other four. Taking the concept in a Western direction, iconic thinkers Carl Jung (psychologist) and John Steinbeck (writer) put a lot of stock in finding one's center as well. For them, the *non-centered mind* is a root cause of much everyday unhappiness and pain. Yet, for them, the centered mind is an antidote to many of these troubles and especially to that of mid-life crisis. This "middle country" of the mind, the fifth season, is the driving force behind all purposeful living. It is your mind's chief executive, coordinating your own energies as they rise and fall, instant by instant, project by project, season by season, year by year. In the coming pages we will see why and how.

Eastern philosophy and holistic arts identify east as the direction of beginning, transformation, and birth. This is the reason traditional martial arts forms (movements that look like dances) as well as a wide variety of other Eastern arts start by facing east, the direction of spring and the new, rising energy.

South is also important and symbolic in Eastern wisdom, so much so that it is given top position on the Chinese compass. It represents summer or the high point of the year.

The pattern of seasons moves from spring to summer to autumn to winter. Late summer is in the center position, extending its continuous influence before, during, and after each of the other cycles. The following chart of this cycle is circular, which indicates the cycle is continuous and each of its seasons and their unique energy are connected and flowing endlessly.

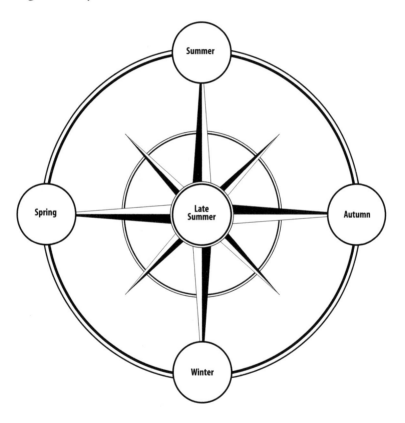

Many answers you seek toward improving your life are found in your ability to harness the ebb and flow of this cycle. It is more than just symbolic. We experience it physically every day as we follow sunrise to sunset and in the waxing and waning of our own body's energies. In fact, we experience it in all that we do. This is because, again, we are not living *with* nature, we are *a living part of it*. Eastern wisdom, holistic arts, and medicine have considered the impact of these cycles on the mind and body for centuries. It is their basis for living well.

The five seasons and the psychological and physiological currency they provide is nature's way of helping you break away from those things that limit your energy, creativity, and capacity to create the life you want. It is nature's way of helping you accept the various changes that come into your life and to live by going with the flow rather than resisting it. The formula is simple: *Change the way you understand and use nature's energy and you will change your life.*

How to Use This Book

The Five Seasons is divided seasonally, exploring the unique natural energy of each season one by one. By the book's end, you will learn how to identify each cycle's energy and how to use it to relieve anger, fear, impatience, aggression, hyperactivity, impulsiveness, moodiness, depression, rejection, over-indulgence, shyness, broken-heartedness, physical weakness, body pain, dependency, memory loss, poor decision-making, and more. You will learn how to sync up your mind and body to nature's cycles and use this connection to keep your mind flowing all day—every day—all year long. Importantly, you will learn how to transfer this flowing mindset to a wide variety of personal, situation-specific daily goals.

You will learn how to flow with the seasons year round and also how to ingrain each season's energy into your mind. Once ingrained, you can then access each season's energy to influence your daily activities, regardless of what season you are in. This will help you achieve everyday balance and task-specific strengths in a wide variety of daily situations. Ultimately you will bring more peace and harmony into your life and will help others do the same.

Each section of the book concludes with exercises intended to help you apply the chapter's main concepts and techniques. To experience the full benefit of these activities, repetition and practice—which is always the hallmark of any good training regimen—are necessary. Thus, the more often you practice, the more benefits you will gain.

You will probably notice upon your first reading that you currently favor and act most from the energy of one of the five seasons. Everyone tends to do this. It's sort of your M.O. The point is, however, not to become anchored to any one season's energy or to nitpick anyone else whose current energy is at a different phase than yours. Rather, try to flow harmoniously with them. Your gift to yourself is what you receive on this journey. Your gift to the world around you is what you give back, without judgment.

For your convenience, the book also includes a glossary of terminology. Most terms that are italicized and bolded in the text are included in the glossary.

May the concepts and the skills presented in the following pages serve you well—as they have me. Enjoy.

SPRING

Every seed is the promise of a thousand forests.
—Deepak Chopra

Change
Beginnings
Upward Mobility
Cleansing
Light
Seeing
Creativity

Spring is a season of surging energy. It is a time of awakening and cheer; a time of light, brightness, and shining. Spring energy, like the sun, is sparkling and explosive, productive, and rising. It is nature's free and vital energy for generating change and new growth.

The spring cycle activates in us and the rest of nature this way for a reason. We have stored in our minds an array of intentions, bundled up with the strategies we used to materialize past achievements, along with new strategies, feelings, thoughts, and the creative energy to help us drive them. We have stored these bundles in our mind all winter, and they are now ready to come out and seed our new year of growth. This forward movement is natural and essential. It is all part of nature's surge to stimulate transformation and grow things.

Spring begins with the *vernal equinox*, which in the Northern Hemisphere is usually on March 20. This is your time to begin making your dreams come true, spreading them like seeds in your everyday world.

In many ways, this cycle functions like a genetic code readying to begin construction, so you have to proceed with awareness and care. Being aware will increase your opportunity to optimize this season's energy and growth with purpose and comfort. It will help you plant the right dreams, in the best place, at the right time.

Clean-Up

You already know that it is often difficult to engender change, even in some of the smallest, idiosyncratic behaviors of your life. Nature also knows this. It is why spring's special energy is so torqued up. It is your power for cleaning up whatever you feel has become messy in your life. What's more, this notion of cleansing applies to physical as well as emotional and spiritual matters.

First, however, you have to clearly see where the mess originates so you can keep it from returning. As you trace problems, conflicts, and disorganization—the mess—you will discover that much stress and unhappiness in your life is the result of what you have learned and things you have come to believe. And these things can knock you out of sync with your environment.

We are all subject to what we think—what we learn, what we feel, what we observe, and what we commit to memory, whether intentionally or not. The human mind is incredibly fertile. You plant a seed in your mind, and it will grow. When you were born, you were a clean slate. Your mind was able to flow unfettered from one thing to another. This is why learning is a joy, a *flow* activity to most young children.

Now an image you have of yourself and the world around you lives in your mind—literally. You don't have little filing cabinets inside your head filled with your personal history; rather, science tells us that the images and memories that are you are electrical currents in your brain and can launch your behaviors in milliseconds. When you say you are "wired" a certain way, this is more literal than you may think. Some of this wiring occurred before you ever saw daylight, while you were still in your mother's womb. After you were born, you began to carve images of yourself, your potentials, and the world around you into your mind at a very early age. In fact, by 3 months of age, you had "downloaded," from every-one and everything in your environment, a vast collection of words, images, opinions, values, and reactions. This was the beginning of your view of the world and your potential. It all began entering your mind without your scrutiny or con-sent. Much of this data lingers to this day and triggers what you may notice as patterns in your life. This is what happens when someone is sitting, say, in a restaurant or café, and has an immediate negative opinion of a total stranger who enters the room dressed in bright-colored shorts and an offbeat T-shirt, but has immediate positive feelings about his new boss who looks more similar to the way he does.

Certain images you carry of yourself in your mind are harmful; for example, that you are stuck in a dead-end job or that you don't have what it takes to accomplish a life-long dream, or that to get along or get ahead you have to sacri-fice who you are. You may feel you have no choice but to either fight or "suck it up." These images are antithetical to spring, but are not immune to its energy for planting seeds—although they keep you stagnant, stuck in limiting ideas and beliefs you never agreed to, you may be re-seeding them year by year. These images can be likened to a computer virus: Just the way a computer virus wants to dictate how your computer operates, harmful images you have of yourself and the world want to run your life. You begin to think that these images are who you really are, and that the world is really this way, and so you start using your energy as well as nature's energy to sustain the image. This behavior is how the mis-alignment of energy and goals meld.

Problems such as ill health and unhappiness can occur from a lack of harmony between your inner needs and your outer actions. The difficulty is that images planted in our mind—without our conscious approval—have convinced us that they should pick our direction for future growth. Just like computer viruses, they are capable of creating havoc in our lives. It is not unusual, in fact, to see individuals aggressively chasing after self-destructive goals in spring. After all, the season will help give you the energy to drive your visions—whether they are in your best interests or not.

Changing this misalignment is essential to changing your life.

Upward Mobility

Spring offers you the momentum for upward mobility. It offers both the raw power and energy dexterity you need to help rid yourself of troublesome self-images, feelings, and actions and replace these with healthier ones you already have in mind or can create for yourself. Use it for this purpose.

Because spring's tendency is to energetically flow toward newness from your core and prune all unnecessary obstacles, this cycle can draw your attention to what's cluttering and clogging your mind. The best clue that something inside your mind is stealing your happiness and drive is if you periodically become aware that you are doing things that are not really you. This could involve your career, relationship(s), familial situation, recreation, creativity, health, and so on. Your awareness of such behaviors urges you to break free of everything that is compromising you. You are feeling this way because the heart is your center for happiness. Spring energy is associated with the heart's own (organic) rising energy. This is your energy for reaching outward and casting your dreams. This is the dynamic energy that is capable of seeding abundance in your life that will be deeply connected to who you really are.

Lawrence was intelligent and pleasant. From elementary school straight through high school and college, he loved exploring science. He attended a good state university where he spent four years studying science. Lawrence was also shy and had difficulty meeting new people. To others, he seemed an introvert, though that wasn't the case. Lawrence would speak more or less depending on how much he already knew a person. And, because of repeated bullying in his early school days, his degree of quietness also depended on what others thought of him. Lawrence was quiet, but he was not relaxed—just the opposite. Spring energy, whether in the actual season of spring or in the "springing" off (launch) of a discussion, event, relationship, or job, would make him feel conflicted. His energy surged, burgeoning with thoughts he wanted to share, but he felt trapped in his choice to remain silent. Inside, he was like lightning with nowhere to ground.

Seeding his own new directions this past spring, Lawrence applied for new employment in the field of business. In particular he liked jobs in organizational communication, similar to careers of several individuals whom he admired. He assumed that such vocations had brought profound satisfaction to their lives, so why not his?

Because he was smart and had impeccable credentials, he landed one of the positions.

CR

Vanessa is in her mid-20s. She had been working for a hometown veterinarian, a friend of her family, ever since she was old enough to work. She went to work at the animal hospital in the first place because she thought of herself as loving and wanted to care for small animals. She will tell you, if she knows you, that she prefers to be around animals most of the time rather than people. So she found her way into just such a situation—where she could be mostly among the tiny creatures she loved as well as around people with similar sensitivities as her own.

Vanessa worked at the hospital until about a year after she finished her undergraduate degree. She was a natural and had her coworkers' respect, but Vanessa had plans.

It seemed to Vanessa that her wings had been tied forever and now she had this burning desire, this "dream" to stretch them out and fly. Flying, for Vanessa, meant freedom. And freedom, for Vanessa, meant flying away from what she had been doing for so long. Spring for Vanessa became all about seeding a different direction.

Know Thyself

Self-awareness is a critical component of achieving freedom. It prevents the things you *perceive* as "just the thing for you" or as momentarily positive or necessary from taking an ironic twist and shackling you instead. Self-awareness gives you a better read of what will be truly right for you and how to exercise your freedom to achieve it, while remaining in harmony with your Self and your world.

At worst, without self-awareness, you will lack, and perhaps find yourself craving, the deeper satisfactions that life delivers when you are doing something meaningful to the person you are and want to be. Feeling a disconnect between who you believe you are and the things you actually do can drive you further away from yourself and into a path of detrimental behavior. Self-awareness at its best will flow you through life, intrinsically rewarded and feeling in harmony with people and goals along your path.

Unfortunately for Lawrence, he was unable to navigate himself to a place of higher esteem and happiness. He managed, instead, to plant himself in someone else's idea of the good life. For Lawrence, this turned out to be a painful experience in which he felt self-conscious regarding his social inhibitions. Floundering, he developed an attitude that he could not succeed, but he soldiered forward anyway, in a job that ran against his grain. Soon, his supervisor (not Lawrence) made the decision to terminate his employment.

Vanessa relocated to a major metropolitan area. She took an apartment and went to work for a high-profile women's cosmetics organization. She enjoyed the distinction of working for a prominent company. After several months of that and some very quiet moments in which she listened to what her feelings were saying, she realized she felt out of balance. She turned her sensitivity inward. She took a good look at the surge of spring "fever" that had rocketed her out of her bearings. She decided to overrule her previous urge to spread her wings and came up with a plan to get herself back on track by seeding a path to veterinary school. Today Vanessa works in her own veterinary clinic where she enjoys interacting with her coworkers and, most importantly, her 4-legged patients.

❧

Spring offers you a way to reset your mind to a healthy state of balance, efficiency, and happiness. Spring, again, is your opportunity for cleaning up—identifying more authentic seeds that have risen from *your* creation, planting them, and watching them grow. In resetting your mind, you can defragment, re-organize, re-create, and reap pleasure from flowing forward with your life. A calm awareness and honesty are key.

Listen to the Message of Wood

Each of the five seasons links to an element that helps you understand how that season's energy works. The behavior of these elements helps you see what to pay attention to in your own behavioral patterns, both within the specific season and in any other moment in life when you are naturally within one of their specific cycles.

Spring is connected to the element of wood. The wood element can help you in your pursuit of more self-awareness and honesty. Unique to wood is its ability to grow upward and downward at once. It is able to establish new growth and yet deepen its roots simultaneously—a process important to human nature as well. Roots nourish your entire organism. Roots are significant in Eastern wisdom because your roots nourish your core. Your core is who you are. Fully charged, your core will defeat the mental viruses living in your mind uninvited. Remember, these viruses are a psychological liability that holds you back. Your core will provide you with a more authentic perspective and guidance to help you target and pursue desired successes. It will refresh you with a profound peace and tranquility while you achieve your goals. Afterward it will reward you for even thinking of such goals, heighten the bar, and amplify your reward.

You are rooted when your mind, body, and spirit fuel and support each other as they work toward the same goals— when they are approved by you. To approve them, you must stay aware. You are in balance when your energies, planning, productivity, and so on are all rooted in who you are at the core and in what your heart desires. Your energies and actions align. You are relaxed, focused, and confident. When you start living from this vantage point, it sends your brain the message that this is how you want to keep living. When you send your brain this communication repeatedly, it ultimately starts going there automatically. The rooted, aware person will generate calm, authentic change that soothes her whole being. In sync with the seasons, you begin to live this way more and more—more automatic, less conflicted, more prizes, and good surprises.

Listen to the Message of Wind

Spring's climatic link is wind—which can be helpful or not, depending on how you use it. Wind can be supportive to wood; it helps it seed. Wind helps wood prune and create new growth. It nourishes. It helps wood flex.

Wind can also be detrimental. It can dry wood to the point of brittleness. It can spread fire. It can snap wood.

The ambition to push too hard is characterized and driven by wind. This ambition can be damaging to you and your goals, during any of the cycles. In the spring cycle, pushing too hard in any direction can prolong a narrow or personalized focus when you may need to keep your attention wide and more objective. You cannot become compulsive about tending to any one seedling as this may result in your neglecting others—and remember, nothing has fully blossomed yet. Your job is to get a plethora of seeds out there.

Anger

Anger is a natural human emotion. Aggression, as well, is normal and healthy. It is the driving force behind much good, creativity, and success. But aggression is an energy that needs to be channeled positively or it can quickly surge out of control.

Consider this: Anger, mixed with positive aggression, can swiftly illuminate your first steps (if you are lucky it can light your whole path) to eliminating an obstacle between you and a current goal. The world of athletics is chock full of great examples of this: We have all seen the Olympic skier whipping down the beautiful white mountainside, beautifully focused, making split-second adjustments, trying to outdo a previously disappointing performance. Or the tennis pro coming back after missing more than one shot with what look like superhuman plays, at lightning speed.

Balanced, this emotion can be channeled into higher, smoother consciousness, focus, and response. Because anger and aggression are so sensitive to spring's rising energy, it is a great time to experiment with channeling emotion toward positive goals.

In contrast, we have all witnessed the opposite effect of this emotion: Mike Tyson's infamous ear-bite on Evander Holyfield in the WBA Boxing Championship in Las Vegas, on June 28, 1997, provides a good example of this kind of energy run amok.

The Message of Personal Pain

Because your mind, body, and spirit participate in nature's cycles, harmonizing your inner and outer worlds and aligning your energies will help keep you healthy and promote healing. Remember how the wood element provides an example of simultaneous upward and downward growth. It is almost paradoxical. Yet, by growing your character, you get closer to your innermost Self. By listening and adjusting your physical and mental circumstances to nature's cycles, you can bring more of your truest nature out in the open and feel more *real*.

Here is the short and sweet of it: Feeling real will snowball— the better you feel about yourself, the better you will feel about the life you are leading and life in general. These feelings will roll over and over and the goodness will grow and flow.

When your mind (your awareness) is too busy to pay attention to the influence of environmental cycles, life's communication often takes the form of personal pain. Nature knows pain is something most humans will eventually listen to. The pain may appear subtly, in the form of stressors and anxieties. This is because stress and anxiety are usually the result of conflict. It doesn't matter if the conflict is *cognitive*, *emotional*, or *energetically systemic*. If you are still too busy to listen, the message gets louder. You then may begin experiencing troublesome dreams, painful life experiences, and emotional and/or physical sickness.

If you are still too busy to listen, sickness may become chronic. Your only choice in the end is to listen and rebalance or be swept away in the downward spin.

It is important to note that the high-surging energy of spring can be used to spark rebalancing or it can become destructive and lead to even further anxiety and pain. Living in harmony with the seasons is preventative medicine against this kind of pain.

Tillie's anxieties had been irritating her like a rock in her shoe since the end-of-the-year holidays. She was stressing at work, and at night couldn't turn her mind off even with a little wine. She found herself getting up in the very early morning, usually around 3 a.m. She would check e-mail on her iPad, look for any new followers on Twitter, and read any tweets she'd received since she fell asleep earlier. She secretly hoped something would magically pop up that would transform her life. Her insomnia worsened and she began getting up twice a night. Finally she started making morning coffee by 4:30 a.m. and she was crashing before even arriving at work. She was exhausted and started having muscle aches in her arms and legs; even her wrists had started hurting. Her glands swelled and she felt congested, not sure if it was her allergies or a cold. Spring hadn't really changed any of that.

It was the beginning of April when the snowstorm hit—over a foot in one night. What a surprise, so late in the season. Tillie woke up to the cold and sparkling white snow. When she found out she had the day off from work, she decided on a leisurely breakfast with her partner. It was also a full breakfast, instead of the usual coffee to go and cereal bar. Her partner put the radio on in the kitchen and made an extra omelet for their Siberian husky, Max. The whole family enjoyed their unexpected time together. That morning when Tillie took Max out for the usual quick "business trip" route, her partner came with them. Having all the time in the world, they let Max lead the way. And he went every which way, steadily unpredictable. The sun came out brightly and the air warmed to a sizzle considering all the snow. They all knew the snow wouldn't last so they stayed out longer, enjoying Max with his furry face whitened from poking it into snow banks. That night Tillie slept well for the first time in months. When she woke up the next day, she felt refreshed. She started thinking about changes she had to make. Thinking this way already started helping her feel better. She looked forward to more.

Sometimes all it takes is a little reminder that there is more than the usual way to do things.

How to Optimize Your Spring Energy

Spring is your time to begin advancing your dreams and torqueing up your energy with the rest of nature's energy. It is also a great time to make those personal changes you have been thinking about.

Syncing up with your environment's robust and rising energy and tuning your mind and body to this momentum will give you the fuel you need for spring work, recreation, socializing, and relaxation. Let the brighter days and bigger sky literally widen your eyes. Let the seething energy you experience with all your senses incite you with bursting brightness, clarity, and fecundity. Enter this forward momentum and flow.

Use spring's potency to move ideas productively and creatively forward. This is your cycle to look for the best ground in which to plant these ideas and grow your dream. Don't limit your searches. Be creative in your searches. Don't push things to grow at unnatural speed or in adverse locations. Don't look with too much expectation. Just look. And don't look so much for endings, not now. Look for the seeds that begin growing. Keep an eye on where each may lead. Be plentiful and diverse in sowing. Widen your focus so you can see it all; execute your actions efficiently, rest, and widen your focus again.

Robinson never thought he had the capacity to invent. He has, however, always been a cross-referencing thinker—in other words, he likes combining ideas the same way he enjoys pushing food around his plate so that it mixes together into novel flavors. Robinson studied literature in college and went to graduate school for a degree in fine arts. But he also loved psychology. He was interested in technology, but mostly in how it could facilitate the arts, not so much the other way around. Robinson recently strolled into Starbucks for his favorite coffee drink, where he planned to sit back and relax. As he sat there sipping his latte, he had a thought. He pulled out his iPhone and checked online for universities that offered degrees in psychology. He wrote down their numbers as though he was gathering seeds. He let his mind flow freely. He wondered if they would allow him to create his own program, combining nanotechnology, fine arts, and philosophy. Robinson had been out of school for 20 years, but he was more excited than ever. When he got home, he started making calls.

Exercises

ဆ **Spend time outside.** The spring cycle begins a time of more light and rebirth. Welcome the abundance of light with your eyes. Feel it with your whole body. On bright days, you can use this high-quality light to soothe and awaken you. Smile with your entire body as it luxuriates in the richness of this purifying light. Smile with your mind. Just being out of doors will begin to activate your body's ability to draw energy from the environment into itself. The more you relax, the more you can feel this activity in your body. So relax. Commit this experience to memory so that you can draw upon it during times of lesser light and lower energies. Try to remember the visual details of your experience right away, within 15 minutes after it has ended. This will send your brain the message that you want to remember it. Think of the details often during the day. This is important because at night your brain rinses out the details of things it thinks you don't need—like the color of the barista's watchband at the coffeehouse you went to that afternoon, or the face of a person exiting a building as you are entering. So you need to tell your brain what to do. When you think of something several times throughout the day, the brain gets the message you want to remember it and sends it to your long-term memory and ingrains it even deeper. The result is that you remember the item and you remember it more quickly. Use your uplifting and relaxing images as needed.

෩ **Visualize images of change in your life.** Spring's dynamic energy enhances these perceptions. Your additional clarity in this cycle can help you identify paths that are good for you and avoid those that aren't. Each feeling, image, and thought you generate carries with it information and a potential lesson. Simply listen and observe. Remember that imaging changes and any newness you want to pursue won't hinder new growth in your life. Only your attitude can interfere.

෩ **Take walks.** Take plenty of walks. Take a deep breath. Go through each of your senses. Experience some element of spring that appeals to each. As your mind drains of stress, consider new projects you may wish to begin. Make this something that you really want to pursue and that it is connected to your honest interests and desires. Pick one and ask:

* Where can I cast the first seeds for this project?

* What preparation do I need before seeding this project?

  Then take action:

* Begin seeding this project.

* Identify the next project and repeat.

෩ **Be positive.** Think and exude positivity. Let spring energy lighten your mind and body. Let its free and rising energy make your mind feel like a dynamo. Believe that you will acquire results.

෩ **See what happens.** Don't push or force results. Your job is to simply observe and see what happens—how, when, where, and why. Add the information from each of these to your *psychological currency*. This way you can become more proficient the next time you are in this energy cycle.

∞ **Be harmonious.** Feel how what is going on with you internally is affecting how things are going and growing externally. Synchronize toward positivity.

∞ **Use spring's variations of light.** Your eyes are great receptors of energy. As this cycle's bath of light enters them, it creates different effects within you. Take note of these effects in the morning, afternoon, and evening. Commit these images and the feelings they arouse to memory. Recall them randomly throughout the day. Also take note of how you are feeling at the moment they first catch your eye. Ask how you are feeling emotionally and physically. Are you rested or tired? Scattered or focused? Are you hungry? ...and so on. Then, ask: What is the effect? This way, the next time you need to send your mind "up" (to energize) or "down" (to relax) you will have some "light" medicine committed to memory. Use as needed.

∞ **Keep a record.** Pay attention to what environmental details affect you positively and those that affect you negatively. You may wish to write them down. Note: Many images will feel different depending on circumstances—such as day of the week, time of day, how much sleep you have gotten, nutrition, your overall mood, other factors in your environment, and the day's events. Include these details in your report. Getting to know your energy needs and responses will allow you to more precisely match physical and emotional goals with the various environmental elements that will promote them. Keep a record of these and put them in your environmental medicine cabinet.

so **Carry your brain in your pocket.** Use your iPod or cell phone to take pictures of natural sceneries that have a calming or energizing affect on you. Later you can view them individually or as a slide show when you need recharging or relaxing.

so **Supercharge spring-like images in your brain.** Let's say, for example, you have a photo on your iPod of a flower garden in your favorite park. When you view it later, try scripting a story in your mind of a time in your past when you felt really comfortable with someone and bring that individual into this garden setting with you. Let yourself interact with this person. Let it play like a movie in your mind. Enjoy the blend of calm yet energetic feelings this activity will spark. (Note: Psychologically, the more parts of the brain you use, the more powerful the effect. For this exercise, you have combined your visual and language centers. So if it is relaxing and energizing at the same time, the effect will amplify, recall faster, and sustain longer.) Use this technique often and carry your best mindsets in your pocket so that when you need them they are there at the push of a button.

so **Learn from nature.** For example, observe the intelligence of new buds pulling energy from the earth to nourish their blossoming. Touch them. Imagine the earth's (and sun's) energy entering them and moving about their fibers. Appreciate them with as many of your senses as possible. Feel the comfort in this nurturing intelligence. Notice new, unexpected growth, like daisies poking out of the ground where last year there were tulips. Let your mind flow to a myriad of new and different thoughts. Observe your thoughts objectively so you can remember them later. Don't judge. Every time your mind takes you to a different place, take a deep breath. Inhale slowly through your nose. Feel the clean, moist energy from the soil enter you through the bottom of your feet with your in-breath. Feel it energize the center of your body. Put your consciousness (mind) there at your center. Don't attach an image; just make yourself sensitive to the energy passing through you. Allow feelings and emotions to bubble up into your consciousness and pass through you. If your mind starts racing, use your eyes to help you focus on those things you have discovered that work as natural relaxers. Let your thoughts and feelings float through you like images on a still lake—light, smooth, and fluid.

Later, pick a few of the details that caught your attention and think of them as communication. Look for patterns in the details and also in any reactions to them. Were you attracted to color, to light, to rapid shifts in climate, to moistness, to warmth? See if you can experience them emotionally again. Specifically identify what emotions as well as what physical sensations you are feeling. These may just be sensations of warmth or cold and feelings of well-being or of anxiousness. Do you see any patterns in the things you were attracted to or in your emotional and physical responses? Ask: What are these patterns suggesting? What changes? What growth?

Later, consider dynamics. What were you powerfully attracted to? What did you powerfully resist? Does your body crave any specific environmental or climatic patterns, or does it resist any? Are there any to which it is indifferent? Each of these is connected to your overall wellness. Cravings and resistances indicate imbalances in needs. Ask yourself what these are suggesting. What can you can hope to learn? What new directions can you seed?

෨ **Consult your intuitions.** They can predict changes in your life before they happen. You can use this clarity to encourage potential forthcoming change that is good for you, edit other changes, and prevent change that is not in your best interests. Don't worry about what may surface into your consciousness as you scan your internal environment. Each feeling, image, and thought can carry with it a lesson. Simply listen and look for the lesson. Remember that imaging changes and newness won't get in your way. Allowing them into your focus is akin to spring chi. Again, only your attitude can interfere. You can also use your intuition to look outside yourself during these quiet moments. Nature has a way of speaking to you when you are paying attention. For example, say your attention keeps diverting to a hawk circling in the distance. Use your eyes to record the entire event. Let your emotions absorb it. Scan the whole picture. Take in as much detail about the hawk and the setting as you can, especially the way you feel about these details. Don't think about anything until later. Just look and enjoy.

Later, do some research about hawks. Record what you find. Hawks, like other species, have differences. See if you can identify the hawk that you observed. What are its special characteristics? Could any of these characteristics be speaking to what you were just realizing about your internal environment? Could any be speaking to your current life concerns? Does this information speak to any recent concerns about your future? Nature has equipped us with feelings because they are great sensors of information vital to our needs and goals. Think about what you were feeling. Were your feelings cool (more detached), warm (mildly connected), or hot (strong)? Ask yourself why. How did your feelings relate to internal concerns? How do they relate to change? What new directions do they suggest?

Later, reflect on how many times nature calls your attention to these same concerns about present and future issues in the next two weeks. Consider each an attempted communication. Write these down. Look for patterns not only in the details themselves but also in what they imply. After you have done some calm thinking and even some research on these subjects, ask yourself what lessons each presents toward helping you grow your future. Again, look for the patterns and listen. Don't be surprised if several are pointing you toward the same exact course of action. Keep an open mind. Stay relaxed and use your newly collected information to help you see and plan. Use spring's rising energy to start seeding your plan.

ဢ **Use music.** Music is a highly effective way to help balance the mind with nature's seasonal energies. Start by identifying songs that enhance your appreciation of the sights and feelings engendered by spring. No type of music is better than another; what matters is that you like the song. The more you like a song, the greater its effects. So pick ones you like a lot. If you like classical music, Mozart's Sonata in D Major (K48) has been lab-tested: Similar to spring, it has a rising energy and has been shown to increase alertness and focus. "These are the Days" by 10,000 Maniacs is another one that many people like adding to their spring playlist, as are "Here Comes the Sun" by George Harrison, or "Every Breath You Take" by the Police. Again, what matters most is that the music you pick is what you like. For you it may be The Knack's "My Sharona," "The Notre Dame Fight Song," or Jennifer Osborn's "If God Were One of Us." Your songs could be classical, techno, rock, jazz, or country.

Once you discover which songs work for you, put them on your iPod, cell phone, or even your alarm clock. Make yourself sensitive to when and where they work. You will find that times, places, moods you're in, and several other factors influence whether the song will have your desired effect—and how much. Set up playlists that match certain songs to very specific situations during this season. This way your brain gets the message that this is where you want your mind to go whenever you enter this specific space—such as your drive into work or when you are about to make an important phone call or when you are waking up and organizing for the day.

Tip: If you want to ramp up an uplifting effect, play something slow first, then follow it with something faster. The faster piece will have a stronger effect and it will last longer.

Use your iPod to make a musical slideshow using some of your playlist songs as a backdrop. Remember, the more parts of the brain you use, the greater and faster you will feel the effect.

ℰ **Use scent.** This can be a stand-alone activity or you can combine it with your iPod slide show. Consider using natural fragrances like spring rain, wild berries, floral and citrus scents, lavender, sandalwood, musk, and amber. Colognes and perfumes you and your partner might use during this season can work wonders. Identify those that have a relaxing effect on you and those that energize you. Use when needed.

ℰ **Think positively.** Positivity affects the amount of energy the body can absorb. It is magnetic. The brighter your attitude, the more and stronger energy you are able to pull from your environment. As your positivity crests, notice how your body and mind enter a state of softness, high-quality energy, and alertness. This mindset will allow you enough flexibility to absorb the most and best of spring's rising energy. Positivity will allow you energetic access when you need it. Negativity restricts access. Let the sensation of spring energy flow into your muscles and mind. Feel it surge. Return it: Send high-quality energy back out into the environment with your feelings, thoughts, and behaviors, and it will return.

ℬ **Use your mind's language center.** List five words or phrases that you associate with positive, cleansing, surging energy (for example, *flow*, *sparkle*, *surge*, *breathe*, *radiate*), and say these words to yourself as you bring more energy into your body and mind. Record how your body feels different once you have nourished it with this energy. List times during the past two weeks when you could have used the benefits of such energy and how it would have made a difference in your overall performance and feelings. Importantly, repeat these words to yourself and anticipate their effects in specifically targeted situations when you need that specific feeling (entering an office meeting, driving home from work, having a delicate conversation with a partner, colleague, or employee). Repeat your "power word(s)" a few times before and after the specific situation. Repetition is how your mind gets the message that this is how you want it to operate and that certain information needs to be placed into long-term storage with fast recall. Once you train your mind to activate in the way you want, it will start doing it all on its own, with or without the words. You can feel positive effects in as little as two weeks and fully conditioned effects in about three months. Later, find songs that contain these or similar words and that will send your mind the message it needs to be hearing for specific situations. Add these to your playlists. Use them often.

ꙮ **Explore spring climatic changes sensually.** For example, if it is morning, feel the air with your skin. Taste it in your mouth. Envision it entering various parts of your body, such as your lungs, blood, and bones. See it traveling through each of your organs. To enhance this, run your in-breaths and out-breaths over each organ one at a time. Feel what physical and emotional effects this generates. Be aware of these effects. Try these activities for each of the various weather conditions common to this season—coldness, coolness, warmth, dampness, wetness, heat. See how each of these affects you. Remember, the more of spring's specific energies you can identify that affect your body and mind, and the better you can match this cycle's energy with your personal goals, the more success and happiness you will engender during this season. Ingrain these in your memory. Use as needed.

ꙮ **Meditate daily.** Set aside time each day to cleanse and *root* your mind. Begin by asking yourself what dreams have been in your heart all winter. Let your mind flow with possibilities of planting your dreams.

ꙮ **Eat less this season.** Try eating only when hungry. Use body-building foods rich in proteins, but in moderation. The same goes for carbohydrates. Excessive proteins or carbohydrates can interfere by inhibiting the quality of your energy flow.

Enjoy cleansing foods such as whole grains, fruits, a variety of green and leafy vegetables, and a variety of herbs and spices.

Sweetness promotes upward energy movement, but, again, think in terms of moderation.

Nature has made it easy by providing you with a built-in color guide to nutrition. Green is the color of choice in spring—try a wide assortment of fragrances, textures, and tastes. This creates a sense of contentment that helps balance body, mind, and soul. Think newness. Spicy and pungent tastes are traditionally known to spark energy you may need to explore different directions.

Everyone must ultimately find his or her own most favorable diet. However, everyone should avoid overeating, processed foods, and toxins. All these dull your energy as well as your ability to invoke, receive, and store environmental chi.

Unused energy can create ailments, so after meals, do some light movement. Problems of misalignment will arise when the body is toxified or your body's internal energy pathways are blocked. Moderate exercise will keep these open.

ॐ

Think light and be light. Like wood, use your energy to stay connected with your core as you begin to branch out in new directions. Let the wind sail your dreams.

How to Correct Spring Imbalances

The way you coordinate yourself and your daily tasks with the seasonal environment can trigger various physical and emotional effects.

For example, spring's rising energy is powerful and upwardly moving. It is extremely refreshing and useful toward the seeding of new goals as well as the expansion of goals already in place—again, whether minute by minute, day by day (micro), or in longer terms, like season by season, year by year (macro), and so on. Yet, when you slip out of sync with this season (or others) you may experience a variety of predictable imbalances. Let's take a look.

The way you experience the environment sensually, for example, can affect your thinking, feelings, and emotions as well as your blood chemistry. It can do things like spike the flow of hormones within your bloodstream. These include dopamine, adrenaline, cortisol, serotonin, and other hormones. All of these changes can then extend their effects, under the radar, throughout the rest of your day, and even longer. They can do you a lot of good and, to be sure, they can also inhibit your performance.

Identifying seasonal imbalances can stop a potential malady ideally before it occurs or at least before it enters a chronic stage.

The new year had kicked off with bang for James. He had begun several projects to make life better for his family (a wife and an 11-year-old child) and himself. But by the time mid-April hit, he already felt like he had bitten off more than he could chew. Frankly, he felt wiped out and generally unhealthy. One of the things he had become obsessed with was extending his family's stint at a vacation property they rented each summer. In order to do that, he wasn't saying no to any professional work he was offered, in addition to his 9-to-5 employment. James had been moonlighting for years, but this year he took it to a whole other level. He just kept his sights fixed on what would come of all of it—a whole month on the beach. He was putting all the effort in for himself, yes, but for his family as well. Although his wife supported his efforts, she was concerned about his health and also the lack of family time. His son, on the other hand, started to feel overlooked, become more demanding, and was showing some attitude.

Looking back, James realized he hadn't gone jogging, which was a passion of his, in at least two months. He was starting to feel he had lost the positive mindset his running provided, as well as the stress-busting. He was more anxious now and had trouble getting up and out of the house in the morning. Paradoxically, he now had to go to work earlier in the mornings to make up for things he wasn't getting finished because of all the extra freelance work. One day, he came home from work, collapsed on the couch, and switched on the television to relax. He heard a loud crash coming from upstairs. When he went to investigate he saw that his son had thrown his bedside lamp into the wall. He'd never done anything quite like that before. Or had he? James realized he didn't know. James thought, *How many signals have I missed lately?* He realized at that moment that something had to change.

Symptoms indicating energy imbalances with the spring energy cycle are usually easy to spot. The most common symptoms are: poor judgment, taking life directions that feel hazardous to your core, feeling mentally scattered, poor planning and organizing, or excessive effort to get things accomplished. It is unrealistic to think that you can stop these entirely at all levels. You can, however, realistically help keep them from becoming chronic and damaging.

During the spring you experience times of altering emotional energies. Just as the spring cycle shifts climatic dispositions often, quickly, and sometimes dramatically, your own moods are potentially subject to varying shifts. The good news is you can use imprints of this cycle's energy, which you have ingrained in memory, to help re-balance.

Exercises

∞ **Conserve energy.** Spring energy is strong, and surges. One reason you may lose energy is that you are more outcome-oriented than simply planting and watching for growth. Spend some time outside. Locate one thing in all the greenery that you enjoy seeing. Spend some time seeing how it harmonizes as the environment, of which it is a part, is bursting into life. Consider ways you could be spreading yourself too thin. Identify ways you might better harmonize with your daily routines and conserve your energy so that there is more to go around.

ॐ **Create high-quality energy.** A martial arts master once said, "Your body is a vessel. It can only hold so much energy. Get rid of the bad and replace it with good." One way you can do this is through physical exercise. Power walking and jogging are great outdoor activities. But you have to like what you are doing. Any sporting activity is good: hiking, rock climbing, tennis, golf, swimming. Because your body can only hold so much energy, the bad energy will dissipate and will be replaced by the good. Of course, this only lasts so long; simply repeat—just don't overdo it or you will become fatigued. The idea is to build up, not break down. (Note: exercise will also increase the energy you need to optimize your focus.)

ॐ **Avoid stagnation.** Stagnation may be the result of putting all of your eggs in one basket—or, in this case, planting all your seeds in one place. Try to put forward a variety of new ideas and dreams that you hope to grow. Stagnation (as well as fatigue) may also be the result of inflexibility. If your mind or body is strongly resisting something, ask yourself what's going on. If there is reason for the resistance and the reason is real, don't force the issue. If the resistance seems *un*reasonable, again, don't let it stalemate you. You can always proceed with caution, collecting more information as you move forward. Take a nice deep breath. Use your images of brightness and warm, moist earth to charge your mind or your energizing spring playlist and/or slide show. Better yet, go outside, even for a moment, and experience spring's uplifting sensory pleasure. Then, think your situation through. Use the traffic light colors: Red means you'll stop and take another path. Yellow means you will proceed with caution until you can determine if the path is right for you. Green means all is clear and reasonable so move ahead. Whichever path you take contains a lesson. Any is new growth.

ꙅꙅ **Avoid frustration.** You have to watch out because frustration can turn to irritation and that can turn to anger or depression. So catching this one early is important. Frustration can come during this cycle from trying to chase after or control too many things you are planting. It is easy to get too ambitious. You need to give yourself a break and rest. Being in nature's rising energy can be deceiving because the energy is so strong. But it can keep you too narrowly focused, fatigue you, and then frustrate you, especially if you become resolute about a single goal or outcome. So keep your focal lens wide. Try to remain objective, for the most part. Of course, if you notice something is damaging or going badly, then you need to prune it to protect all the other potential good.

ꙅꙅ **Control anger.** If you have a short fuse, just like fire in wind, your anger can get out of control fast once attached to rising energies. You need to know your personal signals that tell you that you are *almost* angry, that it is "coming on." For some, it is increased heart rate, shallower breathing, dry mouth, and tightening of the muscles and ligaments. All of these correspond to an imbalance in the spring cycle. If you recognize it, you can divert it. Anger is especially dangerous with rising cycles because of the surplus of energy you feel. Rising energy can be a two-sided blade: One side gets positive things done. The other side hurts and destroys. Know what things calm you down best during this season. Know the signs of entering the "almost" zone because it is then that you can still turn back. Make yourself aware of how you compensate for these "almost" feelings so that you will learn to keep anger away. Some suggestions: The quickest brain-fix is scent—it will bypass your thinking brain and go right to that part of the brain where things can transform in seconds or less. Find a fragrance that calms you down, perhaps in a perfume or cologne or oil, and use it, repeatedly, when you are in calm and relaxed moments. Use color as well. Green is great for calming, as is white. You may have a picture with luscious greens in it that you have ingrained in your memory. Use playlists of natural sounds, or musical playlists. Another easy fix: Try a brief walk outside (or glance outside if time is not permitting), take a good deep breath, and focus on something lovely to you. Smile, and hit your mind's restart button to get back in the game.

so **Shift from negative moods.** Experiment with processing information. When you see someone who feels on top of the world, you'd think you can't help but feel some of that energy, but it doesn't always work out that way. It's up to how you process the details. If you are in a negative mood, for example, you can process someone who is smiling at you as mocking you. Am I asking you to put on rose-tinted glasses? Yes—and no. Don't sugarcoat things and lie to yourself, but choose to flow with the goodness you see, enhance its good feeling by connecting it to other good images and feelings, and flow with that. You can also choose to be neutral, or you can reject it entirely. Your other option is to re-process it into negative energy that will pass through you, take its toll on you, and pass forward to everything in your environment. Your job is to locate and absorb positive energy, enhance it if you can, and pass that forward.

ಏ **Alleviate irritation.** Try taking a walk through a field or park in early morning amidst all the new growth, or watch the sunrise from your front stoop—or, even better, from a location that is new to you. Put yourself in close proximity to these rising energies. Let them awaken newness in you. Let them enhance the goodness you already feel. Experiment. Look closer, deeper, farther, and from new perspectives. As you shift your attention from one thing to another in your environment, feel the subtleties of energy and how they affect you. You can't help but feel this. Just make yourself attentive. Note how each subject you focus on sparks different energy inside you. You may feel warmth that begins in your chest or abdomen and rises upward. You may feel this energy as an emotional reaction such as joy or contentment, or as a sensation of warmth flowing through your body. Let this feeling comfort your body and elevate your mood.

ဢ **Focus.** Sometimes the problem is that you have distractions. These can be pruned if they are not connected to the success of your goals. You can differentiate between those that may be useful in the more distant future and those that you have determined will not be or are damaging now. If you feel that there is anything at all to be gained, you can always put that material on a back burner for a future date.

Other times, the issue with focus is that you have too much energy. For this, you can apply any of the calming techniques we have discussed. Focus issues can also be the result of too little energy. For this, use your energizing techniques. For either of these, if you incorporate various parts of the brain—language, auditory, visual, smell—effects are quicker, amplified, and longer lasting.

ဢ **Reorganize.** Problems with disorganization can result because you are dealing with a wide array of information during this cycle—casting a lot of various types of seed. You may have trouble juggling all this. The surging energy can intensify your disorganization by moving you along uncomfortably fast. So it is important for you to slow down often, rest, take a look at everything that's going on, and reorganize. Keep an ongoing list of things to do that you edit daily, if necessary, and even throughout the day. Be flexible in reorganizing to fit the direction things are taking, and again, prune where necessary to give more time and energy to the best of the new growth. Always be completely honest with yourself, and know that what you are pursuing is indeed authentic to your needs and desires—not someone else's dream or influence, but yours and your future's. Remember the lesson of wood: Like wood, you must grow in new directions and yet with greater roots. All the organization in the world won't generate authenticity. Only when you are self-aware—rooted—can you see what real authenticity is and organize it purposefully.

- **Manage multitasking.** This season's energy can fuel more extreme multitasking, which can frustrate you and deteriorate your focus as well as your memory. So you have to take care not to take on multiple tasks per moment. You can handle some multitasking: that which involves tasks that are closely associated with one another. For example, you are planning what route you will take for a weekend getaway and you are at the same time looking at a map that leads to your destination and naming the various highways to your partner. He is listening and writing the directions down. That's okay. You get into trouble when you are shuffling back and forth from your map to a phone call you are having with your best friend as your partner writes down directions.

- **Give something back to the world.** Help someone else plant a new seed into their future. Or use your skills to help someone through an imbalance this season. This is the best way not only to sharpen your own techniques but also to give back.

How to Cultivate the Spirit of Spring
Meditation

A martial arts master once said to me, "Where the mind goes, your chi goes." What he was trying to explain was how you can absorb and move chi within yourself. His statement has always been the clearest and simplest way for me to understand and convey this process. Take nature's energy in. Let it sooth and enliven you. Channel it to where it can do the most good.

Try this meditation outdoors, or, if you can't get out, via a slide show on your cellphone or other device, or with hardcopy pictures.

Start by taking your shoes off and walking barefoot on the moist spring earth. Feel the cool moisture travel straight through the bottom of your feet. Feel your body absorb energy up from the moist earth.

See this energy circulating within you. See it flowing up over the crown of your head, down your back, and down into the earth again, in a circular motion. See it cleansing you of toxic feelings, as it flows, that may be weighing you down physically and/or mentally. Direct these negative energies down into the earth. See them flowing into the earth. The earth can handle these poisons. You cannot.

Repeat this activity as long as you are comfortable, and do it often. Feel your mind clearing and loosening each time you draw in more energy.

Visualize this energy as a warm, nourishing, vibrant green. Breathe the entire image into your body deeply and slowly, in through your nose, and exhale it through your mouth. Look around your environment or an imagined favorite one.

Now, close your eyes and turn the whole picture green and breathe it all in. See this cleansing energy rising through your limbs, through muscle and bone, to your heart. Feel its rising energy flowing through you. Let it purify and warm your heart. Remember, spring's energy will help flow your heart's deepest dreams outward. As you exhale, see the energy of your dreams flowing outward in peace and joy. Feel the calm exhilaration of consciously participating in this cycle of new beginnings.

Use this meditation to revitalize often.

Resolutions

Spring

- ໑ Today I will spend some time outdoors.
- ໑ Today I will observe nature's intelligence in the new growth of spring.
- ໑ Today I will reflect on my dreams.
- ໑ Today I will begin to spread my dreams like new seeds into my world.
- ໑ Today I will pay attention to how what I believe influenced my important decisions.
- ໑ Today I will stay rooted as I explore new directions.
- ໑ Today I will practice observing rather than influencing.
- ໑ Today I will try to sustain positivity in all that I do.

- ❧ Today I will help someone plant a seed in his or her future.
- ❧ Today I will bow to all of life, acknowledging that it is part of me and I a part of it.

SUMMER

There ought to be gardens
for all months in the year,
in which, severally, things of beauty
may be then in season
—Sir Francis Bacon

Flaring
Maximum Power
Growth
Heart

Fire
Passion
Partnership
Circulation

Summer is a time of abundance and passionate effort—of continued rising energy and heart. It is a time of big sky, warmth, and heat. It is the energy of circulation—physically, mentally, and socially. By synchronizing with this cycle of soaring, hot energy, you will be able to help your physical and mental energies reach maximum potential.

Summer begins with the summer solstice, which in North America is on June 20 or 21, depending on where you live. It is your time to "get out" more. Think about networking. Socialize. Open up to hear what others have to say. Share your own thoughts as well. Think: "More."

As you grow individually this season, everything around you is growing. Think about what you can contribute to your social and work cultures. Consider what they can contribute to your new undertakings.

The summer cycle is largely about making connections: organizing and expanding, whether it is your vitae, business network, meetings and conferences, or time to be with family, friends, and colleagues, especially those you haven't seen in a while. Summer's distinct energy will help you network ideas you have been developing independently during winter and spring. Let others add to your vision. Tap their feedback to help you re-tool and reorganize.

Physically, you may often feel your metabolism spiking during this season. Pay attention to this energy. Make yourself aware: *What good does this energy surge do me? What do I generally accomplish with it?* Ask yourself: *When, where, how is it needed and functional?* Cultivate this energy. Ingrain it in your memory. This way you can access it at times of need, whether during the summer months or any other time of the year.

Flow and Soar

Because summer continues spring's rising momentum, this season will keep your mind alert, flowing, and soaring. It is your time to really put the pedal to the metal. You can accomplish a lot this season. But you want to flow, not race. I say this because a problem with this powerful load of energy is the temptation to rush from one thing to another or to bite off more than you can chew. So keep yourself in check. Enjoy the acceleration—just remember that when you are in flow, you are simultaneously calm and energized. So also check in to be sure that this is how you are feeling: calm and energized. Remember, when you feel this way, your energy is balanced.

You will know when you are slipping out of balance because you will feel stressed, anxious, or rushed. You will lose your sense of calm. Your relaxed mind is vital to staying in flow and to your ability to make accurate decisions within this cycle's escalating wave of energy. Moving in with a balanced mindset will prevent you from burning out, which can happen when you have too narrow a focus, for too long, without fulfillment. It's like spinning your tires in high gear, in the mud. Eventually, things will overload and start shutting down.

We've all made decisions while we are excited about something. These kinds of decisions can be tricky in that there is a tendency to let things go that in more "even" circumstances we would catch. So again, balance is key.

You may discover you have a tendency to wake up a little earlier during this cycle. This is normal. When your mind is in flow, you naturally want to increase your challenges. It often feels good to get an early start. Psychologically speaking, as you begin to see the merit of growing your goals, you feel like raising the bar a little higher. This actually makes it easier to enter and sustain your psychic flow. The process, itself, of growing your life, becomes its own reward. It's no wonder you can sleep less, accomplish more, and feel good all over.

Heart Energy

Summer energy is also the currency of joy. When this cycle's energy is optimized, your heart is strong and warm, and your life is joyful.

A balanced amount of joy, which we know is influenced by the ebb and flow of particular hormones in your bloodstream, will help optimize your focus, memory, self-esteem, and motivation. This is especially important as you age, for many of these hormones will start registering lower on your dipstick. You can, however, use nature's seasonal energies to help keep these hormones flowing. Try to see summer's joy as it blossoms throughout your environment. Make this blossoming part of your personal blossoming and joy.

When balanced—when joy is not overly high or low—it is also good for your circulation: informational, interpersonal, and physical, in terms of the health of your heart itself. As you reap the rewards of better all-round circulation, you will generate more joy throughout your life and create the need for more circulation, and so on. The process loops and is synergistic. And because of this, it is associated with and strengthens your personal link to what is commonly referred to as *the Law of Attraction* (or "like attracts like").

Letting yourself locate and luxuriate in the joys that present themselves in your life will bring you that relaxed, calm, yet stimulated feeling you want in both your mind and body. This is especially necessary in summer when energies can be flaring. The tricky part is learning how to sustain this feeling. Once joy or any of your emotions attaches to the fire element, they can become excessive and dysfunctional, so you need to stay balanced.

Inordinate amounts of joy can lead to delusion and hyper-excited behavior, resulting in rocky thinking, poor decision making, and potentially harmful activity. It can also become addictive, taking you off course as you look for the next fix to make you feel happy. Too little joy, on the other hand, can cause insomnia and fatigue, and lead to depression.

Ultimate joy is realized when what is in your soul and in your everyday life are able to merge.

Try to experience ways to go beyond your "usual" slices of happiness. Get closer to your bliss. This will help you blossom into all that you can be, making your mind clearer and happier and your body healthier.

Your Spiking Aggression

Summer's rising energy, similar to spring's, can spike aggressions. Aggression in itself is neither good nor bad; it is needed to accomplish certain tasks, but sometimes it can be downright destructive. Even positive aggression can sometimes leave you scattered or sapped and lead to blue moods and eventually even depression if you stay in it long enough.

When you process rising energy into over-excitement, you can, at times, feel as though you are on a rollercoaster ride, emotionally and physically, frenzied one moment and fatigued the next, both of which can turn to irritability and then the wrong kind of aggression. The best policy is to be aware.

Use summer's warmth to keep your aggressions in check, and use summer's bright radiance to help bring joy and heart into your play and work. When your daily activities are being performed out of joy, you will be better able to ward off stressors and experience a deeper and more pleasing sleep at the end of your day.

Listen to the Message of Fire

Hottest of the seasons, summer is connected to the element of fire. Fire blazes upward. It gives warmth and helps life blossom. Holistic arts tell us that fire, when it is balanced within you, is a tremendous tool for reaching your goals.

The fire element animates you. It brightens your face and puts a glow in your eyes, gives you bright, healthy skin, heightens your immune system, and helps keep disease at bay. The element of fire keeps your mind sharp and focused. It also increases your sensuality and sexuality and can help keep your weight in check.

Some people are uncomfortable with the aggression this element elevates in them. But when controlled, fire's aggressive energy can refine and quicken decision-making, whether gut-level or counterintuitive. Fire gives you the power of stick-to-it-ness, when you need it, helping you adhere to tasks and concentrate. And it can fuel you as you break down obstacles keeping you from your goals.

Additionally, just as fire's energy promotes the growth of new earth and thus strengthens your roots and deeper Self, it supports the growth of those things associated with your passions or dreams and gives them strength and foundation. The idea is to utilize summer fire, connectivity, and circulation to generate more fertile ground for you to pursue and grow your dream you.

Jocelyn is a recent cancer survivor. Her battle with the disease, as it does for many, awakened the fiery audacity in her that believes it's never too late to pursue your dreams.

At 45 years old, Jocelyn's summer plan is to coordinate several new directions that she had initiated last spring, starting with her fiancé's and her decision to get married in December. So change is in the air. Add to that: The good news that her fiancé has the kind of employment that he can work from anywhere. This makes it possible for them to pick where they want to live. And for Jocelyn it has become possible to pursue another life dream, which is to live in the Rockies. For the couple, this will involve relocation and new employment for Jocelyn (which she has already procured). Both partners know this journey will introduce new people and mentors into their lives. Both want that.

The challenge, for Jocelyn, had not only been only the cancer; it had also been unplugging herself from a family situation that had become toxic. This involved extended family members who had made themselves dependent on her and overindulgent in her generosities of time and money.

She has spent her summer trying her best to remain objective while assessing things honestly both outwardly and inwardly. She and her partner are progressively connecting pieces of longstanding dreams to their new plans like a bridge.

Now they are ready to take charge and headed in the direction of their hearts.

Follow a Natural Imbalance

In Tai Chi there is a continuous back and forth movement. A great Tai Chi master once explained to me that as you begin to move into a posture, you can already feel your energy flowing both ways: forward, and somewhat back to you, and then flowing forward again. He likened this movement to a tractor-trailer filled with water coming to a near stop and the water swaying back and forth as the truck then continues moving forward.

In life, insofar as energy flow is concerned, undesirable events can cause you to lose perspective on your dreams. Yet, this very occurrence will engender in you an increased depth and appreciation of your dream. It will, if you don't ignore it and instead put it to work for you, increase your momentum toward your dream.

The potential consequences of resistance, on the other hand, are frustration, anger, and depression. These emotions can crash in, dissolving your perspective and the places in your mind where there was once the motivation and drive to reach your dreams. Summer's energy can be used to break down barriers positioned between you and your dreams and put you into a mindset powered by heart and the fire of willpower. Then, once you have removed the barriers, your energy will naturally surge forward again.

Here is how it works. All universal movements (such as the seasonal cycles), in which you are a participant, seek balance. If you are in a cycle that promotes growth (such as the summer cycle), when you remove an obstacle that is in your way, you create a reverse action. Some individuals cause this kind of tension in their lives on purpose to intensify their sense of reward once the obstacle is removed: Athletes drive their muscles into failure to promote faster muscle growth; Zen Koans (philosophical riddles) slow your mind to a crawl and then speed up and deepen its growth; some people diet before holidays so that as they allow themselves to "splurge" the reward feels greater; conflicts in the business world can, once dissolved, lead to faster and more innovative product development, stimulate and bond teams, and grow the economy.

If you are losing perspective on a dream, don't resist it. Sometimes you can try going with it. Carefully let the imbalance occur. Then, rest. Step back. See what's going on. Let your fire element build, but keep it in check. Meditate. Exercise. See if you gain your perspective back, perhaps somewhat pruned and reorganized.

Fire Makes Fodder

Fire energy can create more fodder to help grow your dreams. Just as in the environment it can burn wood into new earth, fire can give you the energy you need to help eliminate harmful roots that have grown, with or without your permission, in your life. Once eliminated, similar to the obstacle of Jocelyn's extended family's irresponsible dependence on her, a natural imbalance occurs. This then stimulates more growth in a new direction. Suddenly you are all fueled up with somewhere to go and nothing in the way.

You can also follow your energy the other way. As hard as it may sometimes feel, don't dismiss your body's or your mind's desire to slow down for a bit during the season of bright light and fire. Spread yourself out and chill. Daydream a little. Much good can come from this natural and temporary imbalance. Remember, the expansion of one creates a need for the other, and each will adjust. Time you spend strategically doing "nothing" here will fuel the fire you need to accelerate (as well as help re-seed) and continue growing later. So give yourself some intentional rests and pauses as a natural part of your journey.

Mind on Fire

In **holistic psychology**, memory, thinking-power, and consciousness can all be associated with the fire element of summer's energy cycle. In Western science, we also know that you have to reach a certain level of energy for optimum mental and physical performance. Consciousness works similarly.

Consciousness is like a powerful Wi-Fi within your brain. It is a field of awareness capable of receiving information from all of your brain's networks. You are able to regulate this incoming information with what is known as your brain's executive function. So you can use your brain's **C-Suite** to, in short, consciously choose the way you think, feel, and act. You can choose, in effect, to hold off on something your mind and body are momentarily craving, for something less subtle that you are able to perceive is in your better interests. This executive decision making is what allows you to set (or re-set) all of your mind-power to match situations and goals with optimum performance.

When your mind is flowing, the fire element is high. Your willpower is strong. Your energy feels luscious and smooth as you fluidly sail from one task to another. Your mind is free and open and happy. Your movement and decisions feel easy and accurate. Your mental acuity is peaked. Summer's seasonal power throws your C-Suite into high gear. It gives you the wherewithal to bloom—and to keep blooming—a whole new mind. And thus, a whole new you!

How to Optimize Summer Energy

Summer is all about syncing up with nature's continued rising energy. It is a time of robust outward energy and activity. It is your cycle to expand and coordinate the pieces of your life that you planted in the spring. Your job is to observe these elements of your life and watch them as they blossom. Summer gives you the energy to nurture all those that blossom in a positive direction and are truly meaningful to your heart, your dreams. It also gives you the energy you need to clearly identify those that are dysfunctional and prune them.

The summer cycle is associated with the emotion of joy and connected to the rising energy (outward-bound dreams) of the heart. When these are balanced, you are able to flow in a direction you feel is authentic and important to your life.

Summer is linked to the element of fire, which drives your maximum outward engagement as well as your sense of focus, logic, coordination, and organization. When all of these components are in balance you feel your optimum physical, cognitive, and emotional strength. You are relaxed. Your mind is flowing and alert. Your heart is warm and happy.

Alicia never had trouble sleeping...until one summer. If you asked her why, she would admit she had a lot going on, but it wasn't just that. She was also anxiously waiting for something to happen—for anything to come from all the effort she had put forth since the beginning of the year. She and her husband had been trying to conceive, but so far, nothing. They had also been trying to sell their home. They had already put a down payment on a new one, in a new neighborhood they wanted to raise their child in someday soon. It seemed to her that nothing was working out. Her mantra became, "I need to hear some good news." Her husband, who tried to soothe her, would say to her "A watched pot never boils."

Alicia never really took her eye off the "pot," so to speak. Her insomnia, however, was sending her a direct message that she needed to cool down. So she put less emphasis on watching. Instead, she made a short list of things she loved to do in the summer months. These were little things, not big—things like jogging; tending her garden; time at the beach, where she would relax to the sound of the ocean waves; day trips on the weekends into the neighboring state; and nightly meditation, something new for her, to help her de-stress and get more satisfying sleep. She emphasized these things instead. Although she couldn't wipe her mind clean of her goals, she increased her level of joy—which cooled off some of the fire in her mind and body. By late autumn, both major bits of news she had been awaiting arrived.

Exercises

ઠ **Stay balanced.** Keep a relaxed yet activated mindset for your daily routines and make some time to be outdoors.

      Use summer's abundant light. The summer cycle continues your time for more natural light. As you did during spring, welcome this continued wealth of light with your eyes. Whether you are indoors or out, feel summer's warmth with your whole body. Use this warmth to soothe. Let it loosen you up, body first and then mentally as well. The more flexible you feel, the more all your potentials will flourish. Let summer's light soothe your body. Focus on where inside your body you feel any rigidity.

      Cool down. In Asian medicine, there are layers of cool and warm energies throughout the body. So, for example, you may feel heat on your skin (or coolness, depending on the seasonal cycle), yet if you sharpen your awareness you can send your focus below the skin and find a pocket of coolness. You can also keep moving your focus inward. If you go to the next layer below, you can locate a pocket of warmth, and then, if you keep going, the coolness within that. You can use your visualizations and your breath to guide the comfort you need (coolness or warmth) to the areas where you need it. Just take a deep, relaxing breath and envision it going right to that spot. Remember the adage: Where the mind goes, your chi flows. It may take several breaths to achieve the exact comfort you want, but you can get there.

      Warm up. Spend time basking in summer warmth. Feel it in your muscles and joints. Ingrain this in your memory so you can tap into it whenever you need to, any time of day or year.

🔊 **Heat up.** Ingrain summer's flaring, high-powered energy in your mind. Start by feeling it with your body. Use the color red in your visualizations of summer energy flowing through you. Make yourself sensitive to how this energy makes you feel—physically, mentally, and spiritually—and double up your visualizations by including color. This ingrains its effects deeper into your memory and will quicken its recall and activation as you need it.

🔊 **Observe nature.** Enjoy a wide range of summer elements like rain, the lavish greenness, the plethora of flowers, the water, the breeze, and the wind. Let yourself experience the coolness of morning, hotness of midday, and coolness later at night. Listen to the night creatures and their unique sounds. You can listen to them one at a time or collectively as if they were orchestrated. You may like to listen to the birds at night singing their young a lullaby or sending their messages out through the environment. Morning is another good time to listen. You may like to watch birds soar in the brightness of the sky. Make time to experience this, especially in quietude. You will be surprised how many ideas and solutions can come to you this way—without stress, without your probing or asking or getting compulsive.

🔊 **Go to the beach.** Enjoy the coolness of the water and make sure to commit it to your memory. Feel the heat of the sand. Let it soak into your body and dissolve your tensions. Ingrain that feeling in your mind. Look for the brightness of the water within the darker waves. Imagine the water's coolness absorbing some of the overheated and overexcited pockets within your body (and mind). Use your breath to guide this image. Ingrain these feelings in your memory so you can call them up and use them down the line.

so **Watch a sunrise and sunset.** Ocean sunrises and sunsets are as spectacular as they are in mountains and prairies—or really anywhere. Consider how your physical and psychic energies follow a similar arc, per moment, per situation, per day, per year, and so on. Ingrain this visual in your memory. You may like to photograph the images so that you have them for later. This way you can share them (and their energy) with loved-ones, to make memories and also to help guide their energy when they need it.

so **Create imagery of joy.** Look for and see joy in the natural environment. For you, this may be a trip to your favorite park, a place in the countryside, the mountains, or the beach. Perhaps it is being outside after dark and looking at star-studded night sky.

Don't rely on just your eyes. Use your mind-vision to see the joy, sort of the way a musician might picture the notes of a melody. Continuing the music analogy, there are many other ways to see music—and energy. For example, let's say you are listening to your favorite instrumental. What images does it conjure up in your mind? What if, instead of seeing pictures or images of things, you instead let yourself see a swirl of energy? Try this: Picture the joy you are witnessing—for example, a flower bud that has recently opened—as you might visualize light energy.

Play with the color of the light you are seeing in your mind. Observe it. Make it red, the color associated with summer energy. What if it were in the night sky? What might this light look like? How would it be moving, swirling? What if it could dance? What would the dance look like? What would the music be?

Breathe this light image in and throughout your body. In Chinese the word *ming* means "bright." When you say it twice, *ming-ming*, it means "very bright." The brightness is not just what you might see in a bright light, for example, but a brightness of both sound and light. In Chinese *ming* refers to "sound and light" as one simultaneous thing: sound-light. There really is no such concept in English. So ming-ming is the flash in your mind of both auditory and visual stimulation as one thing.

Play with this energy of joy on the canvas of your mind like a laser show or let it flow throughout your mind-body like breath as you breathe in and out. Locate something joyous in the environment; see it this way, as ming-ming. Hear it. Breathe it. Repeat this visualization often to ingrain both the sound and visuals into your mind. Remember, the more parts of your brain you use, the better you will store the information and the better you will recall it when you need it.

∞ **Use music and literature.** There are so many great songs (instrumentals and lyrical) that are about the joy in our environment. Make a playlist and bring the music with you. Or find a poem that you like that references an aspect of nature that brings you joy and carry a copy with you. Make a playlist of readings of your favorite poems. Put them on your iPod or cell phone. Use these to help enhance your pleasure.

ഐ **Walk in the cool morning.** Or try an athletic activity you enjoy: jogging, tennis, swimming, and so on. Let it soothe you and pull the excess heat of stressors out. This will incorporate yet another part of the brain— that part that involves motor skills—and will ingrain this cycle's energy in your mind even further.

Feel your mind and body balancing the coolness and warmth. Remember that feeling so that you can practice it later to balance yourself in moments and months ahead. Pull the coolness in and let it balance internal tension that may be the result of lingering heated or compulsive thoughts, worries, and anxieties. Feel the coolness lightening things up, rinsing your focus clearer. Breathe in the cool air. Let it cool your body internally. Imagine it flowing through your body until you feel supple and relaxed, yet energized.

ഐ **Use heat to de-stress.** Midday is your best time to feel this cycle's energy peaking. Let it take the tension from you. Bring its warmth—via breath and visualization—to wherever in your body you feel the effects of tension.

If you need a jump-start, visualize summer's energy surging up from the ground, down from above, and in from all around, and let it fuel your fire and flare it to full. Use this clean, surging energy to get out of any doldrums.

Shortly after midday is a good time to start connecting dots from information you have gathered. Bring the contract you wrote up in the morning with you to lunch when you meet your new client and nail it. Take the information you gathered all morning to write a professional presentation and now write it. This is your window to hit your targets dead-on.

ↇ **Amplify summer energy.** Use different parts of your brain to help you ingrain the effects of summer's rising energy. Try plenty of movement (sport, Tai Chi, yoga, walking, gardening), music, pictures, and scents (natural and otherwise—perfumes, colognes, even scents like sunblock and moistening creams and oils). These will lock summer's rising energy in your memory and help you unlock it faster whenever you need it.

ↇ **Use a slide show.** Record your best images of summer (audios, videos, photos) and combine with a musical soundtrack you either recorded during these summery moments or one you made later that, for you, connects. Put one favorite calming show and one energizing show on your iPod or cellphone so you will have it during the months ahead whenever you need a boost of calming or alerting energy.

ↇ **Meditate daily.** Imagine (and feel) summer's high energy flowing through you like breath flows through a flute. Pay particular attention to it as it warms your heart and enlivens it with joy. Let this joy circulate through your whole body and mind. Imagine any stressors leaving your mind and body when you exhale. Use your breathing to guide them out.

- **Know your limits.** It is easy in this season to become anxious to get results. After all, you are putting a lot of effort into things. Sometimes anxieties and compulsions come from feeling that you are not dealing with certain matters. Don't punish yourself and wind up using this great surging energy to run yourself into the ground. Instead, detach a little, eat well, skim off some worry-energy with exercise or physical activity, re-charge with positive energy, reach out to friends, and use relaxing techniques. Sometimes answers can come to you by happenstance. These are just as good and less costly for you. Whether you have to find solutions or they find you, you will need to balance and re-charge as you go forward. Then, when opportunity arises, you will be in the best position to see your goal and act upon it.

- **Push your limits.** Identify something in your life you want to change. Use your summer's surging energy to get you there. Make a list of ways you can begin to put that change into motion. Stay positive. Start right away. Stay on track. Stay balanced.

- **Keep a record.** You will surely have your favorite things to do, but other things may come into play as your season rolls on. You'll know what worked and what didn't, and you'll have made observations—why you think one thing worked and something else didn't. What made a certain activity work better? When you see a pattern, you'll have an important piece of information about yourself—for example, *This works when I am having a bad day at work, but not when I have had a bad day at home.* Use this information to improve your techniques and activities next time around.

ॐ **Cool off—inside out.** At night, find the cooler energy within you and channel it to cool off externally.

   As afternoon progresses and you feel your own
energy and nature's beginning to wane, you will discover a lot of creative ideas bubbling up into your
consciousness. Relax and give some attention to
these. This is a great time of day to see all kinds of
ways you can re-tool the day's events and information
to better hit your goals or drive them to new places.
It is one of the best times of day to problem-solve.
But don't ruminate. Just unwind. Kick back and observe the details as if they were reflections on top of
a clear mountain lake. Then, later, think about how
they might piece together. But, again, don't over-do
it.

   If it is a cool night, go outside or open a window.
Visualize the dark coolness. If it is a damp or wet
night let the water temper and balance tensions. Find
where the day's stressors are welled up in your body.
You will be able to feel tightness—usually in your
chest area, shoulders, back, and sometimes legs. Cool
yourself down.

ॐ **Listen to nature's night-sounds.** Sometimes it is
fun and relaxing to open your window at night and
listen to the music of the night creatures. You may
choose to hear them as a melodic symphony or, at
other times, simply like white noise. Listen to the
rhythms. Feel them. With your mind, attach the waning, cooler energy of night to the sounds. Bring that
slower, calmer energy inward to unwind your body
as well as any psychological heaviness.

૭ **Eat light.** Pay attention to how different foods and diets make you feel. What you are going for is feeling simultaneously calm and energized. Not too much one way or the other. Many foods provide a cooling effect, and TCM encourages you to use these during the hot season, especially if you are feeling too jumpy or stressed. Increase consumption of cool foods to help keep the body moist and strong and the mind calmer. Watermelon, cucumber, and celery are all recommended. Salads work very well, as do raw veggies.

Use more water, teas, especially green tea, floral teas, and mints like peppermint. These cooling foods help cleanse the body. Fish is a good summer choice for a main meal and will help you avoid fattier, greasier meals.

Use moderation. Too much of any foods, even seasonal ones, can easily cause indigestion during this period. Be sure to get enough protein to maintain your higher energy. This will vary per individual. I personally try to keep the carbs down, as too many make me feel sluggish. I do, however, like natural carbs, the kind you get in fruits and vegetables. Check out green juices and assortments of vegetable-and-fruit-combo drinks.

Eat light and use your spices to aid in warding off potential digestion issues connected with the element of fire. It is important to be hydrated. Try to stay cool in order to balance and also to call forth your yin energy.

Do what feels right to you. You will either feel balanced (relaxed and energized) or you will discover you are tipping too far one way or the other. In that case, adjust.

How to Correct Summer Imbalances

Imbalances during this season, particularly over-excitement and depression, can be the result of runaway expectations or exuberance. You may feel so much "fire" and joy one day that you can't possibly match it again the next. Say you have a perfect-10 day—you have perfect weather, you hit all the items on your to-do list right out of the park, you reach out to others and are well received, and everything runs above expectations. Your next day may be better than normal yet again, but not as high over the norm. So you work hard, putting a lot of expectations on yourself to match or better the altitude of the previous day. This time, instead of feeling the above-average day you're having, you will, on the other hand, feel somewhat depressed.

Too much excitement (attached to summer's rising energy and heat) can lead to dysfunctional and even dangerous behaviors, as well as other problematic issues including digestive difficulties, insomnia, increased emotional irritation, distraction, increased worry, stress, anxiety, mania, and depression.

You can sense these imbalances coming and head them off at the pass before they become problems, or, if they do, catch them early enough to turn them around.

One of Robert's favorite places in the world is a river in the backwoods of Massachusetts. It is a narrow waterway concealed between mountains and miles of plush evergreens. Getting down to its banks is work. Depending on your entry, you might have to scale gargantuan rocks, slippery, muddy embankments, or wet, exposed tangles of tree roots. But it was worth it for Robert because it was his way of getting back in tune whenever he felt disorganized or overwhelmed by summer's heat. One summer, he brought his youngest daughter, Victoria, then 2 years old, hiking to the river with him all summer long. He had read that ingraining nature's calming and energizing sounds and colors at an early age could last a lifetime. You'd have the effect in your back pocket, so to speak, whenever you needed it. *What a gift*, he thought, and decided he would help his daughter acquire it.

Now, Victoria is 6 years old. She has a recording of the actual water sounds she and her dad listened to when she was 2 and then again when she was 3, and every so often after that. It has engendered a great calmness in Victoria. She hardly needs the recording at all, and says she only needs to hear the tranquil and cooling sounds of the water in her mind, where they are ingrained. She can also get to that special calmness in her mind by visualizing the evergreens that were part of her hikes to down to the river. The gift her dad had hoped to give her was real. It is has become a great de-stressing tool for those rough-and-tumble moments—for both Robert and Victoria.

Exercises

ဢ **Use summer heat to ease aggressions.** Some aggressive behavior can be as dysfunctional as sun poisoning. Whether dealing with your own aggression or another's, you can use summer heat to keep balance. Try the following: For one day, whenever you catch yourself becoming negatively aggressive or angry, take a pause. Step back and observe. Don't fight or resist your feelings. Instead, ask: *What am I feeling, exactly? Why?* If there are others involved, ask: *What might they be feeling? How can I use this to gauge a response that will advance my goals and best harmonize with them?* Whatever you do, don't telegraph your feelings. Let them flow out of you like water through a hose. Watch as a myriad of solutions begin to bubble up to help resolve the problem. See what a few minutes of calm can do. Leave that faucet on.

ဢ **Avoid urges to micro-manage or over-control.** With these types of focus you run the risk of losing access to important information as well as losing the social camaraderie necessary to keep a team organized, energized, and cooperative. Another danger is that in becoming impatient and narrowly focused, you become pigeon-holed, and your focus fatigues and then burns out. Step back. Take a breath and balance. Then, ask yourself: *Why do I feel the need to micro-manage? Is the need real? Is my approach responsible? What has happened in the past under similar conditions? Respond in your best interests.*

ꙮ **Balance depression.** Use morning's big, clear sky and ascending brightness to open your focus wide. Let it literally widen your eyes as you look far off into the horizon. Feel the coolness of the morning air on your face and the rest of your body. Let it focus your attention on the present. Use your breath to draw this coolness inward and cool off any pressures or worries. Look around at the world in bloom. Watch the sun pouring light over the hills or flaming in the bay or across the harbor, the massive hawk bending into the wind, the barking joy of dogs exploring the rosy scent of another dawn. Listen to the bird-songs. Repeat their rhythms in your mind. Smell the air in bloom. Breathe this whole picture in. Feel it opening the windows of your mind and body—one here, one there, all of you. Ingrain this feeling. Think about it randomly throughout the day when you need a lift. Imagine a red filter, the color of alertness and summer, over the entire scene. Take a long, slow breath and breathe the whole fiery image into your mind and body. Recall this image often to help drive its invigorating energy deeper into your memory.

ꙮ **Balance over-excitement and insomnia.** Use the chill of later evening/nighttime air. Watch the sun slide down the sky, the shades of orange, red, purple, blue, and black—and use these natural images to slow yourself down. Relax, clear your mind, and meditate on these natural, calming transitions.

Revisit this meditation (with movement if possible), especially when it gets totally dark, under the moon and stars. Slow walks, stretching routines, dance, or Tai Chi and Yoga are all good forms of movement to use.

- **Watch a moonrise**, relaxing and staying for the whole thing. This is especially good over the mountains or water. Ingrain in your memory the slowness of this natural pace, mixed in with summer heat. Again, combine with movement when possible. Be sure to empty your mind of all thoughts and negativity as you engage.

- **Use color.** Green is highly relaxing, as is white. Psychologically *and* physiologically, colors have the capacity to alter your moods, dispositions, and cognitive energy. I recommend that you use colored paper. You can also use your favorite photos in magazines or art books. Be creative: Use your iPod or cell phone to take close-up photos of greens and whites as they appear in your favorite natural environments. Then try making a slide show on your device so that you will have these images whenever you need them. You can also make prints of these and place the pictures in a room you like to meditate in. Center your vision on an image as you clear your mind of any thought or negative feeling. You can try taking your heart rate and blood pressure after a few minutes to see which color works best.

ဢ **Use your calming playlist.** Slow, instrumental music works best, but really any songs you like a lot and that will deeply relax you are good to include. If you have one that really works, put that on repeat. Natural-sound recordings (purchased or homemade) also work very well. You can even use recordings of happy, comforting lullabies your parents may have played for you or sung to you, particularly those that your mother sang. Some people have recordings of songs their children sang when they were very young. These are wonderfully calming. Any of these can become your own personal lullaby. Use this playlist only at night so your mind gets the message that you want it to take you to sleep. This way it will begin to send you there more automatically as you enter your room at night.

ဢ **Release "Type-A" energy.** Especially during the summer cycle, be cognizant of adding a few moments of calm whenever exerting a lot of energy for long and steady periods of time. Enhance with any of the calming images or sounds from previous exercises. **Alternate:** Gently rub your breastbone. Draw your focus to your heartbeat. Take slow, steady breaths—in through your nose, out through your mouth. Slowly count backward from 10. Repeat if necessary. End by hearing your favorite summer's calming sound (sound of waves, a campfire, a breeze, whatever you like, in your mind). **Alternate:** Your calming playlist works great here.

ↇ **Balance scattered-ness and disorganization.** First use any of the summer energizing activities in this chapter. Then, try these:

❋ Make sure the spaces around you are organized and tidy, especially in this cycle. Outdoor clean-up is great. Begin the day by watering flowers, pruning a bush, or caring for your vegetable garden or lawn if you have the time. Any of these help organize the mind and put your mind into an organizing mode. This can then transfer into whatever is next on your daily agenda.

❋ Use music. Make an organizing playlist with songs that have the right tempo and rhythm and that send you the right message and mood.

❋ Use songs from times in your past when you were keenly optimized, organized, and feeling completely on top of your game. For you this may be a rise-and-shine march song that streamed over the speakers when you were at camp as a child and had to jet into an organized mindset. Or it may be the tune you and your soccer team used to rally before games. These work great even years later.

❋ Drain some of your energy the night before or the day before you need to be doing work to get everything nicely organized for the next day—including your clothes, breakfast, work materials, iPod, car (if you will need it), and so on. You'll thank yourself for the easy sendoff the next morning.

∞ **Relieve heartache.** If you feel your heart is closed or in sadness, remember a time when you felt the contentment of love and compassion and were safe. Let yourself feel all the particulars. Draw this energy throughout yourself. Let yourself feel it. Feel a soothing energy return, even if momentarily. Use this mental scenario to challenge and reverse your feelings whenever they recur. Consistency is important. With repetition, you can reverse a broken heart.

Try this visualization: Breathe in through your nose and out through your mouth. See the air as a clean, pure-white fog. Make an "s" sound as you exhale. See your breath exhaling pure, clean, and white, taking with it any negative energy inside you. Focus completely on the hissing sound, using it as a distraction of sorts. This will take your mind away from any emotional pain inside you. Repeat as long as you are comfortable and until you rebalance. Do often.

How to Cultivate the Spirit of Summer

A Summer Meditation

The following meditation can be used to heighten this cycle's spiritual energies and awareness. You can practice it in stillness or with movement—that is, seated, or jogging, gardening, walking, or what have you.

Start by relaxing yourself. When you feel calm, let your consciousness sink down to the area where your heart is located. In the *chakra system* (your internal energy centers), this is where your *heart chakra* (heart energy center) is located. In this practice, remember, where your thoughts go your mind will flow, and where your mind goes your energy will follow.

Try to quiet your mind. It's not easy, but try to stop thinking for a little while. This will put your mind and heart together, free and open, on a highway, so to speak, that you can take anywhere.

Breathe slowly and deeply and use your breath to stimulate your conscious energy. Feel your breast fill with energy. Direct this energy nonspecifically outward into the environment by projecting your awareness there. In other words, let your breath guide your consciousness, as if it could enter the breath itself and follow it out. Share your joy with everything in the environment. Feel its joy return to you as you breathe in. Take deep, refreshing breaths and draw that energy into yourself through all your limbs en route to that area around your heart chakra. Let it flow back into your environment.

Do this often. Remember the feeling of such joy. Nature does not speak English, but what it has to say is not beyond your feeling and understanding. Listen into the stillness and silence of all things visible and invisible. Let them bring you joy and balance.

Resolutions

Summer

- Today I will spend time outdoors and look for the rising joy in nature.
- Today whenever I get anxious I will step back and recall the joys in nature.

- so Today I will look for new directions I planted in spring and observe how they are blossoming.

- so Today I will check which of these new directions are closest to my heart and think of ways I can nourish these.

- so Today I will observe a sunrise and ingrain in my memory its fluid, brilliant, and rising energy.

- so Today I will tap my good aggression. I will use it to help circulate my new directions. I will move with a strong, calm, and fluid resolve.

- so Today I will remember to pause and re-charge in between exerted efforts.

- so Today I will practice using my internal "coolness" to stave away heated situations.

- so Today I will try to keep a warm heart and joyful spirit.

- so Today I will compliment a new and growing development in someone's life.

LATE SUMMER

When the soul strips off
its created nature,
there flashes out
its uncreated prototype.
—Meister Eckhart

Transitional Energy
Empathy
Center
Identity

Self
Nature's Core
Your Core

Imagine yourself at the very center of the universe, your arms and legs extended in an **X**-shape, perfectly balanced, as if you are in the center of a great circle, happy, safe, in sync with everything, strong yet flexible, flowing in the momentum fluidly and smoothly, each of the seasons and their specific energies evolving with you, around you, through you, and each of them in a great, sparkling dance of pure energy.

Late summer is you—at the center of everything. Late summer is everything in the universe at the center of you.

Late summer is the middle season, the fifth season. It is the headquarters of it all. When I say *all*, I mean it literally. This is because late summer is the energy that resides at nature's energetic *core* and it is also the energy that resides at the center of your being. This is the zero point at which we are all connected, mind-body-spirit—nature-Universe (God, Universal Consciousness). And it is no accident that late summer is set as the *hub* of everything. Some philosophers would go so far as to call it the seat of the soul.

Located at the center of all the other cycles (see the image on the next page), late summer's presence is always there and always connected to each of the other cycles, providing nourishment, safety, and purpose.

Energetically, it is a cycle full of empathy. In fact, your empathy peaks during this cycle. There is a reason for this:

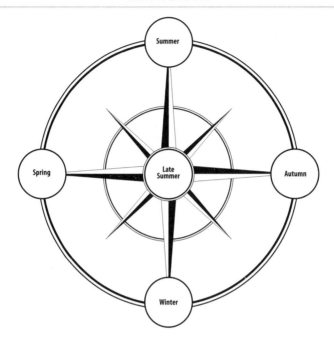

Your empathy peaks at this time because it is essential to keeping your physical and mental energy in balance with your life's pursuits as well as the world you live in. You can choose, for example, to be in sync with this movement, you can choose to be obliviously out of sync, or you can intentionally choose to fight against it. It is your power of empathy, however, that senses who *you* are, who *others* are, and who and what *the world around you* is, and that will inform your choice. But the choice remains yours.

This brings us to the most crucial point in this book, which, at its core, asks you to synchronize your mind and body with the rising and falling energies of nature and therefore of your own moment-by-moment life. In doing so, you will live healthier, happier, and more harmoniously.

Self-awareness provides the key to successfully living this way. Your power of empathy will help give you accurate reads. The more self-aware you can become, the more you will see the person you are at your deepest. Coordinating and organizing your external world to match who you are will enable you to live more peacefully and purposefully. This is why late summer is your headquarters. This is why late summer is the CEO of your mind.

A Time of Reflection

The *2012 Farmer's Almanac* defines late summer, or, as some of us know it, *Indian summer*, as: "A phrase most North Americans use to describe an unseasonably warm and sunny patch of weather during autumn." The phenomenon is generally observed anywhere from mid-October to early November and normally occurs after the first frost. Warm temperatures are usually accompanied by dry, hazy conditions.

A more general notion of late summer refers to those last moments of warm weather and abundant light we experience any time from September to November, before the cold weather arrives. These summery days can last from a couple of days to more than a week, and you may see a similar trend a few times before hitting winter.

Like summer, late summer mornings are cool, though getting cooler. Midday is warm and sometimes hot, and the sun puts a golden glaze on everything. Nights are dark and getting progressively cooler.

During this cycle, it is common to experience the desire for quietude and internal stillness. This is because these components enable you to access the awareness you will need to make fluid and meaningful transitions from one season to the next or from any life-situation to another.

Because this cycle's energy fuels pensiveness, late summer is a good time for a lot of reflection. It is a time of deeper thinking and soul searching. This is the kind of self-awareness iconic psychologist/philosopher William James spoke of when he explained that such focus is at the very root of human judgment, character, and will. It is, according to James, what allows you to take possession of the mind.

Making the time for reflection during this seasonal cycle pays off big. Late summer's energy fuels your ability to process information logically. It helps shape information into wisdom, fueling your spirit with increased energy, self-awareness, and happiness.

Jack finds he easily gets swept away by his disappointments. When he does, he often becomes destructively angry.

This past spring, Jack had a few big goals in mind. One of his goals was to change his career to something that would place his trajectory at a higher, more rewarding level. He had wanted such a change for some time, and he decided to make a goal of trying to land it this year.

Jack is competent at his current job, and gets along well enough with coworkers, but feels bored much of the time. He considers his best talents untapped at work—or worse, unnoticed.

A few years back, he began to prepare for a shift in career by starting a part-time, online graduate degree. He finished it this summer, the prospect of which sparked his excitement in spring. Also during the summer, he reached out to make more connections in the new field he was hoping to enter.

One of his connections was with an already established professional in that field who likes Jack a lot and sees a place for him in his organization. Jack, on the other hand, for as long as he can remember, has had a hard time working with positivity that comes from others.

As a child, his father's dominance was excessive, trying to micromanage much of Jack's life. His father was usually unsympathetic and often hostile. This chipped away at Jack's self-confidence and left him needy. To this day, his father tends to tell Jack how to think—and feel—about things, rather than trying to see how Jack views his own thinking and feelings, and, perhaps, why.

As he grew, Jack desired the support he had not enjoyed from others as a child, and he found himself expecting to achieve it from relationships, particularly those at work. Jack now becomes easily dependent on his friends and colleagues, and in some cases inappropriately attached. He wants support. He also filibusters whenever he meets with friends and associates and tends to dominate conversation with them. He has become a master of shutting down the opinions he, in fact, so desires. Shutting down these opinions makes him feel safe. On the other hand, it shuts him off from potentially important feedback he could use to better craft his path to new employment. When these relationships don't reach Jack's expectations for support, he becomes fearful of rejection and often anxious. Then he becomes angry.

Strategically, late summer is all about keeping you moving harmoniously forward from the rising active energies of spring and summer into the cooler, calmer energies of autumn and winter. In Asian health sciences, this season is your ultimate compass!

Both healthy self-satisfaction and its opposite, neediness, are connected to the way you process the energy of late summer. For Jack, late summer began, this year, by activating his compulsions and neediness. Would he be able to regain his bearings? Could he turn things around to his advantage?

Establishing Harmony

Harmony begins with the desire to take control of your proverbial ship. What's interesting is that the more you take control of yourself, the easier it becomes to harmonize your goals with others.

In his book *The Tipping Point*, Malcolm Gladwell talks about shaping the details and events of one's life so that they result in a huge coordinated event he likens to a tsunami (as opposed to a small storm). This is the difference between arranging events separately for separate outcomes and coordinating them all so that the outcome is synergistic.

Centering helps bring this kind of positive, personal synergy into your life. This is because, centered, you can work the process as a single interconnected movement, growing and moving forward to generate huge (tsunami-like) success and happiness.

Back to Jack: he was right on course knowing that he needed a change in career. He was also on track in beginning his scaffold to achieve it with a graduate degree and then befriending a professional who could help him toward his goal. Unfortunately for Jack, his triggers for neediness fired up and got in the way. He developed high expectations that his newly found friend would mentor him and even offer him employment. But the Jack of old, fearing rejection, began to dominate every conversation. When his friend did not respond the way he was hoping, Jack became disappointed and then angry, and then began to withdraw. His attempt at tapping into his friend's expertise and guidance failed.

Accurate self-awareness helps focus your mind on your real needs, and if you can keep your mind there, on them, you will be able to see solutions as they present themselves in your daily life. Part of becoming self-aware is focusing on your strengths and on any positive details, events, and people that have come your way. But self-awareness also must include being able to clearly identify your shortcomings as well as situations and reactions in which you are unreasonable. Jack had completed half the job and left old triggers behind to activate again and keep him from making it to the finish line.

Sometimes a solution may become observable only for seconds. And so, again, you must also be present and open. The self-aware, present, and open individual will be at an advantage.

Alexandria (Alex) is a 23-year-old business manager. Her closest friends, whom she admitted had influence on her overall world views as well as career choices, had chosen to enter the professions of law, education, and medicine. These all required advanced college degrees, which Alex felt no inclination to pursue.

She didn't take her "difference" lightly. In fact, it made her look deeper into her own experiences and desires. She did a lot of soul-searching via meditation, which she usually practiced twice a day, once in morning and again at night before retiring for the day. Her approach was basically to calm herself down and discover more about herself.

Alex would imagine scenarios in which she felt engaged and inspired. She allowed for different directions to pop into her mind. As she brought up her skills and interests, she allowed herself to see them traveling new paths where they might be used in new ways. What was important for her was that "change" be engaging and more challenging than her current employment. She began to create her own strategy for change. She remained non-committal, but observant.

Alex tried to focus on what she felt she was missing, what might bring greater satisfaction: Did she have deep interest in directions she had not yet pursued? Would she require new skills to go after any of these? If, so how would she achieve them?

She found the late summer cycle to be conducive to this goal, which she made mostly about finding out more of who she really was. *Why start something—anything—you may not be happy with?* she thought. Some individuals spend years pursuing things that leave them empty. She kept coming back to images of herself married to James, her fiancé, with whom she had been in relationship for three years. She truly loved him and he nourished real needs. She wanted a family, and she didn't want to wait long to begin one.

Alex is also a visual artist. She is creative and her mind loves the time she spends in creative endeavors. She feels better physically when she is engaged in these. She is outgoing and amiable and can work with others as well as on her own, and she has real skill with listening to others' goals and extrapolating their purpose clearly and simply. But her bigger skill is in successfully communicating that to others. So she saw herself as someone who can creatively launch a PR campaign for almost any organization.

Alex is a good example of what self-awareness can accomplish in less than a year's time. She decided against any more higher education, at least for the time being. Instead she decided to look for employment opportunities in PR. She found a good one with an organization and individuals that she deemed a good match for her skills and personality. She is now looking into doing the bulk of her work from her own home office, which will allow her more freedom, she believes, in starting a family. But this part of her plan is still on the back burner, as she wants to settle in more to her new employment and upcoming marriage first. The important thing is that her life feels on track and is becoming increasingly more satisfying. She feels strong and competent, and it shows in her composure and in her relaxed and spirited exchanges with people.

Listen to the Message of Earth

Late summer is associated with the earth element and the message of earth, which, again, not only composes the center of the seasonal cycles but *your* center (literally and figuratively) as well. This positioning gives you the perspective you need to develop guiding posts for your life on a road of purpose, organization, and rich satisfaction. Like the mother that nourishes, earth energy in TCM nourishes the mind-body-soul so that they move synchronously. You are sure-footed and rooted in this element. From here, you stand centered among yourself, the world you live in, and heaven (whatever your personal idea of heaven may be). Here, all you have been, where you are presently, and where you would like to be headed intersect.

As in our previous example, Alex, at her point of decision making, followed her core vision, what the mythologist Joseph Campbell defines as your place of bliss.

You can do this too. Begin by asking yourself:

- ๑ How do I respond to conflict?
- ๑ How do I respond to pressure?
- ๑ How do I respond to change?
- ๑ What makes me think and act irrationally? Or: When do I get irrational?
- ๑ Under what conditions do I perform my happiest and best work?
- ๑ What are my passions and dreams?

Your Mind's Filtering Mechanism

When any of us are at this point of searching within ourselves, it will help to prepare for truly letting go of the various things that have come into your life that are dysfunctional and that can hold you back. Alex was sure-footed and self-confident. She wasn't taken in by any need to compete with her friends' academic pursuits. She was connected with who she is, her real desires, and the direction she wants to be headed. And she began building her future from there. It wasn't so for Jack.

Being able to phase certain things out of your field of consideration is important for good focus. This is called "good inhibition," and it allows you to focus on something not because you are narrowing your vision to that one item, but rather because you are excluding everything else you deem irrelevant so that the real subject of your interest remains crystal clear. Remember, just because "stuff" enters your life, that does not obligate you to focus on it, pursue it, and respond to it—nor should you if it is detrimental to you physically, mentally, or spiritually.

Late summer is your mind's filtering mechanism. It will show you what to inhibit because it is damaging to who you are. It will also show you what to activate because you will find it functional and rewarding.

Hanna is 52. Similar to most of us, her mind was filled with ideas as she sailed into springtime this year. One of her ideas was to open a business. She had several other new projects in mind as well and set out to look into the ones that made the most sense to her, at the time. This idea was to open a yoga school. Hanna had been practicing yoga most of her adult life and found it worthwhile in terms of personal health and in enlivening her spirit, but it was also rewarding for her socially.

She decided, after doing some research into all that it would take to try to start her school as a business, that she would be better off taking her time and beginning a yoga club instead. She thought that strategically taking it slow at first would give her the opportunity to see, introspectively, as well as externally, if she wanted to grow the club into a full-scale business. At this point in her journey, she didn't see why not, but decided to pursue things in a more relaxed way instead of jumping right in.

By the time summer hit, she had connected with a women's group at a local athletic club. The group was very interested in having Hanna pilot her yoga club within their already established organization—if Hanna was willing to run the entire operation herself, on a voluntary basis. Considering this a good testing ground to see if her idea for a yoga school was doable, she accepted.

By the end of summer, Hanna discovered that her other responsibilities were wearying once combined with the rigid schedule of running the yoga club. But that wasn't her major discovery. She also realized she didn't like running the whole show by herself. Her original goal of running the club to get more excitement and fulfillment in her life was just not happening. In fact, it felt that in many ways the club was more of disappointment than her everyday job because she loved practicing yoga by herself, but this was more than she wanted to handle and for no payment.

She did not give up her quest for new employment. She did decide, however, that more inner searching into what she might successfully pursue would be necessary. This didn't bother her because she felt rewarded by preventing herself from making a double-big mistake in giving up her regular employment and then starting with something that would not have been in her best interests.

Find Your Center

Confucius said, "Always stay close to center." Late summer's energy prepares you to do just that. It gets you into a hunker-down mode and readies you for the continued falling energies of autumn and winter. But there is an even deeper association with this season's energy, because it is connected to your core or center. Psychologically this refers to that part of you we call the *Self*.

One way to understand Self is to consider it the sum of all your personal traits. Another way to see it is as *pure awareness*— that part of your mind that is self-aware. You can feel this at will. Try it now. Put your focus on that part of your mind that can literally watch you—objectively—as you read these words. It may take more than one try, but you can do it.

In traditional Eastern thought this location is synchronous with what philosophers and scientists refer to as the center of everything: you, your spirit, the Universe, everything in the universe, *Universal Consciousness*, or God.

Being centered in Eastern tradition is a coveted and sacred space. When you place your focus on your center, you are in the middle of it all, you are fully you, and fully a part of all else. Centering is key to purposeful decision-making and activity. Interestingly, the word *China* means middle, middle kingdom, and center.

Knowing Yourself

Through our emerging awareness of Self we can gain more self-regulation in terms of our own thoughts, feelings, and actions, including the way we respond to others. We can develop a clearer sense of purpose in our lives and more strategically organize ourselves to achieve it.

Try this test. Avoid answering ambiguously. Do you feel...

- ❧ Aspects of your lifestyle that have given you a sense of purpose and satisfaction for a long time are suddenly leaving you dissatisfied or empty?

- ❧ Boredom with various parts of your life, from employment to relationships?

- ❧ A sense of confusion or questioning with the general direction your life is headed?

- ❧ Dispirited, uninspired participation with the main elements in your life?

- ❧ A craving for adventure?

If you answer *yes* to any of these questions, you may be feeling the onset of what we refer to as a *midlife crisis (which can really happen at any age)*. But psychologically, this so called "crisis" can have a silver lining, putting you on a quest to find wholeness in your life, a journey that, when successful, will take you to the core or center of your being. It will shine light on what you need to do to synchronize your inner and outer worlds, as well as grow them in a direction of self-fulfillment and happiness, and ultimately become the person you were born to be.

Such wholeness can be considered a "spiritual" (non-denominational) quest of sorts. To many artists and psychologists, the crisis of mid-life is nothing less than a search for one's soul, that part of you born into this physical realm, now lost or left along the way, but still wanting to fully become who you really are.

Unfortunately, late (or Indian) summer falls at a time of year when you are caught up in the hectic and scrambling pace of having to ready for end-of-the-year "stuff." But do you move toward a more contemplative thought process? So often the answer to this question is no. This is because much of what we believe asks us to hustle, and hustle even more, rather than take the time to slow down and become more self-aware.

If you follow this season's falling energy, it will help you avoid the holiday hustle and guide you, instead, to a more centered pace. Slowing down, you will be able to examine how you are feeling and how options that have blossomed into your environment fit in—or not. You will feel less boxed in, less stressed. This translates into a more relaxed approach to life and better, more aware self-management.

A short while after deciding not to pursue her yoga school, Hanna was invited to offer a workshop in yoga at her local elementary school. The workshop was a real success as far as the school, the students, their parents, and Hanna were concerned. As a result, she began to investigate a plan to offer a similar workshop, also for elementary school students, in her town's Creative Arts Center. She had let her experiences, passions, skills, and inspirations open this path for her. Her students and their parents were motivated by her teaching and caring. Consequently, staff at the Creative Arts Center got behind the project, and they were willing to market the classes, which evolved into the yoga school Hanna had originally wanted.

Everything flourished: the center and its personnel, the yoga school, the students (and parents), the additional instructors that were eventually required, and Hanna, whose healthy self-awareness had generated an environment nourishing to all. Plus, she got paid!

Optimizing Late Summer Energy

Late summer is your time to open your heart to who you are—and keep it open. This season's energy will stream you into the headquarters of your Self. Operating from this mindset will facilitate all your transitions—seasonal and otherwise. The main ingredient is self-awareness.

Stay balanced. In order to do this, stay cool, and be flexible; don't' let yourself get overly concerned with goals or expectations, or they can fire you up into compulsive thinking. This happens when you just can't stop thinking about something that has you (and your energy) blocked and you feel like you're searching for the proverbial needle in a haystack. You wind up fatigued and, in the end, unable to focus on anything much.

So stay centered, keep moving forward with your vision, and use the excitement of meaningful self-discovery to keep you flowing.

Sierra is 30-something, single, and feels as though she is wasting away with a dead-end job at the city library. She has an associate degree in

Liberal Arts, which she earned at her local community college.

Sierra comes from a family of five children: three biological and two step children from her father's former marriage. She is the middle sibling. Sierra describes her childhood as having been a rollercoaster ride. Her mother was a heavy drinker and Sierra's perception of her was that she was more attuned to her alcohol than she was to her children. She saw herself in many ways as lucky to have gotten as far as she had, degree in hand, job with so-so pay, and enough all around to get by. But she dreamed of more.

Most individuals who know her say that she is an excellent communicator. She sees this attribute in herself and enjoys her social and professional endeavors.

She also sees herself as over-qualified for her job, which requires no college training. Most of her peers at the library, in fact, have neither higher education nor interest in pursuing it. She doesn't see herself as better than anybody, just unhappy with what she is doing.

Let yourself be pensive during the late summer cycle. This will help increase your self-esteem and strength, and help you feel stable.

These feelings of self-awareness can cause you to draw the line with some individuals who have been dysfunctional and harmful to your inner development. It can also help you limit how their thoughts and actions can invade both your outer and inner worlds.

On the flip side, you might also find yourself forming new and stronger relationships with people who nurture new directions you are steering toward. Let yourself follow these trails. Open your eyes and mind and see them clearly. See how you relate to and nurture each other. Consider what can be done to further this relationship.

> Sierra wound up disassociating from various members of her family as well as some individuals from her work at the library. She drew the line with individuals she felt were holding her back— those who lacked compassion, understanding, and encouragement for her. She found that she was attracted to others who did show her these qualities. This was the opposite of what she had had growing up, and it was something she was now learning to do for herself. Her former lack of self-awareness had kept her from tapping into positivity—her own as well as her environment's, or anyone else's. But now she will tell you that things are changing.

Exercises

ဆ **Keep an open heart.** If your heart feels shut or is shutting down, you cannot ignore it. Take a look at what's going on. Then ask: *Why am I doing this? Why am I feeling this?* Focusing on your actions will be a first step in gaining self-regulation. Ask: *Am I* *trying to avoid something, some feeling? Am I substituting? What happens to me as a result? How do these consequences fit in with my greater goals? Well? Not so well? Do they bring me closer, make me safer, or keep me from acquiring important information or experiences I need to get to the next step? Am I doing what I do for the right reasons? Do I feel "owing"? Controlled? Am I trying to control? What do these tell me about myself? What needs to change, if anything, based on past experience? What do I want to nurture?*

ॐ **Make time to get out.** Let the cool, crisper air of late summer charge and revitalize your mind. Feel it, especially as you begin to rev up your day. Morning exercise is great during this season, but if you can only exercise later in the day, any time is good.

ॐ **Experience this season's reds, yellows, greens, and wide assortment of other colors.** Draw or print squares of the different colors (colored paper and close-up color photos work well too). Set them strategically in your office or at home or carry them in your wallet or handbag. You can use these to help you shift out of mood swings or to adjust the energy you are feeling so that it is more appropriate for certain tasks. All you have to do is take them out and focus on them. As you do, take a clean breath of air, relax, and play a narrative in your mind that is based on a memory of your time outside. See as many of the details as you can with your mind's eye. Remember, the more parts of your mind you combine to form your mental narrative (visual, verbal, auditory) the better and more long-lasting the effect. Center and ask yourself what you need to do to align yourself with your immediate goals.

🔊 **Experience nature's thermostat.** Experience and feel the day beginning in coolness that transitions into warmth, often heat, then declines into coolness and sometimes cold. Remember, late summer is the season of smooth and meaningful transition.

Ask:

* What physical, emotional, and spiritual things can I do better in coolness?

* What things can I do better in warmth?

* What things can I do better in heat?

* What makes me uncomfortable in each of these temperatures?

* Locate that place in your center (your body's location of late summer), and from there practice making transitions from coolness, to warmth, to heat with your mind and literally feeling the momentary changes in your body. You can do this anytime, anywhere, to better adapt to and gain perspective on a situation. Try using this technique few times during your day. Try to refine this with practice.

* Later, turn on the heat in your home, apartment, or car temporarily. Feel that, and remember the transition from cool to warm. See yourself in it as you feel it, as though you are looking through yellow-tinted lenses. Commit this image and feeling to memory. Call it to mind as needed throughout the day to help you rebalance and

transition more comfortably from one activity to another.

ဆ **Try to discover yellow,** in its many hues, in as many natural settings as you can (leaves, flowers, water hues and reflections, grasses, fruit, vegetables, the sky and horizon, and many other locations). Associate this color with the physical feelings of transition you experience in the natural environment as well as within exercises like the previous one. Associate it with a feeling of balance and ability to transition in complete harmony. Store this in your memory as a quick anchor to harmonious transition whenever you need it.

ဆ **Practice transitioning.** Indian summer mornings are bright, with clear blue skies, and you can feel the chill in the air. Trees are turning color. In some places they have reached their peak color. You can see a leaf spinning down in a breeze or wind, but you can still drive with the windows down. Let the coolness blow through your hair and on your skin. Seek the feeling of warmth underneath. Practice moving your thoughts from cool to warm and feeling the transition. Or from hot to warm to cool. You can do this at will. Next time you are stuck in traffic, try using your internal energy to mentally transition you to a cooler place. Take a deep, relaxing breath, and center.

ဆ **Let yourself stretch out and think. Relax and center.** Keep one eye on the variety of things you are still pulling together from summer initiatives. Keep the other eye on your deeper self and if and how these things can nurture who you are.

ɞ **Stay up late.** It's okay to stay up a little later, as you did in summer. Let yourself feel some of the chill at night. Let yourself feel the need for covers in bed. Stay sensitive to the comforting feeling of transitioning from cool/cold to warm. Remember that feeling for when you will need it in your activities. Use this stay-up time to reminisce on all you have done thus far in the year. Don't, however, belabor it. Just let yourself observe it. Center, and consider how details connect (or do not connect) to who you are at this cycle's deeper level.

ɞ **Go out at night.** Feel night's cool chill. Let it re-balance internal spaces in you where you feel frenzied, hurried, and disconnected. Let yourself feel that creative energy within this rich, dark, and empty space. Let the darkness loosen and relax your mind. Ingrain these feelings in your memory. Tap into this feeling throughout the day when you need to step back.

ɞ **Rise early.** Again, immerse yourself in the feeling of transitional energy. Center first. Then, practice smoothing your movement, passing from dark to light, coolness to warmth, and from lower energy to higher. This will help train your mind to automatically behave this way in daily routines during any season.

ɞ **Use morning's coolness.** Let yourself feel this energy shift, from summer's heat to late summer's early morning chill. This coolness helps center and sharpen your mind. By starting out your day in coolness, you can engender the sharp morning focus you need. Commit the feeling to memory. Start using it throughout the day, as needed, to snap you into a focused, centered mindset.

ᔔ **Make yourself empathetic to others.** Listening and responding to others' needs will slow you down and make you more sensitive, which will provide you with a rewarding feeling. Bonding with others makes you feel good and lowers your own feelings of stress. Gauge responses by centering first. As a bonus, you will also learn to better identify and respond to your own centered needs.

ᔔ **Let late summer nurture you year-round.** Each of the seasons gives you the opportunity to memorize its energy and call upon it whenever you need it. Just as spring nurtures summer and summer's energy continues to nurture you now, this season will nurture you year-round as well. It is your guiding force.

ᔔ **Monitor your nutrition.** This season is associated with sweetness. Eat sweet foods to help keep energy high: root veggies such as carrots and beets (more of these), apples, peaches, plums, sweet berries such as cherries, melons, sweeter juices, and stewed fruits. Cucumber and corn are especially good, and squashes, corn, ginger, and pumpkin are all welcome add-ins to help provide warmth as well as sweetness. Various natural syrups can also be used in moderation. In this cycle you don't want to run the risk of extinguishing your energy, so avoid overdoing the sweet fluids. Also watch out for too many hot spices, caffeine, or energy drinks when you are feeling tired, as they can worsen fatigue. Chamomile teas and ginger are good. Try to avoid missing meals, as you will need the nutritional oomph and balance. Eat peacefully and in a relaxed state, and protect your centeredness.

Don't overeat, and keep up your exercise routines to retain high energy and give you a break from too much thinking. You will need that to balance against too much reflection. Don't eat when you are emotional or highly engaged. Slow down. Eat slowly. Be light.

This is your time to slow yourself down enough so you can see and act more clearly from who you are. Be thoughtful, stay flexible, and find your sweet spot.

How to Correct Late Summer Imbalances

During late summer, the mind and body experience the turning point in which nature's rising energy transitions into the cooler (declining) energy of autumn. Even though this is a cycle we associate with peacefulness and calm, imbalances during this season can leave you feeling the opposite—needy, worrisome, and compulsive. Anxieties can turn into *emotional swings* and *disassociation*, which can then worsen as days get darker and colder.

Imbalances during this season can further result in overextension and, on the other end of the spectrum, disinterest. Summer's high-energy activity can, in contrast to autumn's imminent falling energy, leave you feeling bored or flat-lined. You may find yourself, for example, turning outward instead of inward, and over-extending to be entertained or to feel security from others, rather than empathetic toward others and yourself.

If these imbalances increase, you may experience feelings of isolation and loneliness. Imbalances can also exhibit in dysfunctional or aggressively destructive behaviors in your interpersonal and employment relationships as well as within other areas of day-to-day activity.

Heather would tell you that she is a summer person. Her favorite time of year is right before the summer solstice when the days are longest and brightest.

Heather works in a bookstore, where she has been employed for about 10 years. She took the job right after she had recuperated from a serious surgery and was trying to remove all stressors from her life. Her recuperation was successful and within a few years after her surgery, she married. She remains happy in her relationship. She made herself two promises, however, before her surgery: (1) That if all was successful, she would never go back to the grind of secondary teaching, where she had spent more than a decade after earning a graduate degree in English. She still enjoys participating in theoretical discussions involving education, yet says she could never return to the stress that is as much a part of it as its highest highs. (2) That she would live true to herself. When she first said this, she had an idea of what it meant, but lately she isn't sure anymore, as she is conflicted between seeking out things that she might find more interesting and making a living to put food on the table.

She secretly wishes she could do something more exciting and more connected with her talents, perhaps in literature, but doesn't know what that "something" would be. She is bright, likes working with others, and is very capable of materializing ideas into action. Whenever something has come up at work that requires these skills and she has had the opportunity to shine, she has risen to the occasion. But afterward, she has a difficult time getting back to the normal pace of things. The stress she has attempted to avoid creeps up and leaves her disappointed and her self-esteem low.

She doesn't like late summer. She just can't get into the decline to darkening afternoons and cold nights ahead. These elements remind her that yet another year has gone by, and she is still in the same place. She often feels depressed and sometimes lost. She wonders if there is any way to rise above it all.

CR

Bob is a speech therapist, working in a school district not far from New York City. He goes into the city often and enjoys the animation it offers. He is a high-energy person. He usually takes off all summer and travels to fun places with his fiancée. Even so, the pleasure of summer solstice, for Bob, is interrupted yearly with thoughts of autumn's approach. This tendency stresses him out, right in the middle of vacations. He knows it is ironic and unreasonable and self-imposed, but he says that, nonetheless, he can't help feeling this way. He admits that he transitions roughly each year.

What Bob doesn't notice is that he transitions with difficulty whenever and wherever things are not in sync with his expectations and his "high" drains off to normal again. When this happens— it could be any time of day or year—he detaches from others and sometimes feels disengaged for days. He can't stop himself from thinking about the worst of things even during the best of times.

During these downward spirals, Bob gets apathetic. He is often late for clinical sessions with speech clients and meetings with colleagues. It is easy (and common) for him to forget about timely materials, and he frequently will turn them in late. Sometimes he finds himself depressed. Paradoxically, even though he has less energy, he finds himself craving sweets and rich foods.

Bob notices that this time of year his apartment starts getting messier and so does his wardrobe. He feels like the Jackson Browne song, "Running on Empty."

To remedy the situation, he parties a lot, yet he doesn't see it that way; he just sees this as a good time of year to celebrate hard. This energizes him and gives him something to look forward to. He is, however, aware that his partying doesn't work very well in the long term. It only makes his mind-set worse because it knocks his compass further off tasks he needs to accomplish—those things that keep him feeling good for the long run. Then, he becomes irritated with himself and others, and that throws his daily management skills even further out of whack.

Holistic arts maintain that knowing and nurturing who you are is essential to personal strength, health, and happiness. This allows you to use your talents to best interrelate with your environment and others. Because you feel strong and comfortable with the person you are, you are able to go to others for additional support when you need it—and they to you.

Both Hanna and Bob experience a lack of self-awareness. This manifests in imbalances associated with late summer. But that's not all bad news. Although the price of imbalance can be troublesome, it can also function as an alarm to help prevent more serious issues down the line.

Let's take a closer look at the imbalances associated with the late summer cycle and how this cycle's energy can be used to soothe you back into a more harmonious state.

Exercises

∞ **Re-balance.** Feel solid. Get on the ground. Rock climb, hike, roll around or sit in the leaves, enjoy a campfire, have a blanket picnic in the park. The point is to literally feel the earth beneath you.

ℬ **Reverse feelings of dissatisfaction.** It's easy to slip into feeling dissatisfied during this season. You can still feel the effect of summer's hot pace and high expectations. You may think that production or outcomes should have been higher. You may wish that you had created more opportunity. Many of us put a lot of emphasis on certain aspects of growth and take our eye off of other components that sprouted in the cycle. You can feel unhappy when highlighted growth doesn't occur. As a result, some individuals push even harder to achieve what they wanted, so they soldier on for "that one thing" even as energies decline.

Let's start by taking a slow walk in cool morning air to clear out your mind. Dress warm, but not too warm. Feel the coolness awakening your mind. Try to relax and widen your focus without expectation or judgment. Take another look at what's going on. See what differences have arisen within the preceding cycles: start with yourself. Ask: How have I changed? How have my desires changed? Why? Have my feelings or my logic changed? Has my everyday environment changed? How? Why?

Step back and take a look. See how various differences in your life that have arisen—and they will be there—can creatively fit together.

ℬ **Smooth daily transitions.** See or feel nature's transitions at strategic points throughout the day. Try to experience them viscerally. You can, for example, store in memory a visual of a cool, foggy morning dissolving into warmth and sun, then into midday heat and brightness, to a golden, cooler afternoon, and a darkening, even cooler evening, into a velvety black, cold, starry night. Commit this to memory. Consider using your other senses. The idea is to repeat this process many times, as if replaying a slide show in your mind, in order to build a habit of transitioning smoothly. Consider how this momentum can be applied to your daily routines. Apply it first in your mind and then in reality. Once you develop the habit, it will be worth the effort as you will begin to transition more evenly and automatically. It will be like having a little computer chip in your mind that fires whenever you need to shift.

ꙮ **Reverse feelings of detachment and irritation.** Pay attention to the early signals that you are detaching from a situation. You want to catch yourself at the "almost" stage if possible. Then, try this very simple technique and see if you can shift your attention back on track (remember, where your mind goes your energy flows): Recall the feeling you have stored in memory of this cycle's coldness. Now is the time to tap into it. As you do, touch the tip of your tongue to the roof of your mouth—just another way to help shift. Breathe slowly in through your nose. Concentrate on centering. Bring the feeling of seasonal coolness into your mind. Use your in-breath to help you visualize the cold welling up in your center and at the crown of your head. Now imagine drawing more coolness right up through the earth, through the bottom of your feet straight up the center of your body and to the crown of your head. Let it orbit down in front of you and back up several times until you feel revitalized and better focused.

ഔ **Prune impractical or dysfunctional ideas.** During the spring you seeded a wide variety of prospective new directions. During summer, you have grown them. You can now, in late summer, see that some of these directions have blossomed in ways close to your core desires and needs. You can do this with a self-scan.

Ask:

* What new directions and projects have I taken on since summer began?

* With which of my inner desires is each connected?

* How will this desire lead me to a happier, more successful place?

* How does it fit in with other demands of relationship, family, workplace, finances, and living?

* What other essential elements need to be considered and achieved in order to accomplish this project?

* How do I feel about putting more time, effort, and creative thinking into this project?

* Have I pursued something like this before?

* Is there anything I'd like to change about my approach?

✳ What are the potential liabilities of this project?

✳ What are the potential rewards?

Your job will be to harvest the projects that seem best for you at this moment, and, later, to begin to creatively scaffold them toward the future you want for yourself.

℘ **Reverse feeling disorganized.** Prioritize. Take a close look at what opportunity has developed throughout the past cycles.

Ask:

✳ What do I want from this project or situation I feel compelled to pursue?

✳ What specific desires or needs are compelling me?

✳ Do any of these drives influence me to act irrationally, now or in the past?

✳ What do others expect me to gain from this project or pursuit?

✳ What am I currently doing to work toward this goal?

✳ What am I feeling emotionally as I work toward this goal?

✳ Do my feelings move me forward or hold me back? How about in the past?

✳ How do my feelings affect others? Use your own feelings to help you gauge how others feel.

✳ Is this a good course for me to take now?

Don't underestimate goals you may leave on the back burner. Often, if any of these are truly connected to the person you are, they will come up again—until they make it to the top of your list. This is natural and perfectly fine.

ⓢ **Reverse the stress of your changes, in others.** Help others accept your changes. Change will cause stress for others. But you can help other people acknowledge how your decisions may affect them and work with these individuals to help them acclimate. Don't forget, change will affect you too with a certain amount of stress. This gives you all the more reason to utilize balancing activities to keep yourself relaxed and happy and on top of your game. By helping others you can enhance your sensitivity and sharpen your responses to changes you yourself endure.

ⓢ **Reverse your worry.** You may find yourself ruminating about how things will be changing, if changes will work out, and what happens if they do not. These are all legitimate concerns. Yet, you should try to calm them.

First, rebalance your mind. Decide if you need to bring yourself up or down, and apply the appropriate techniques.

Get physical. Increase exercise—outdoors if possible. One of the greatest benefits of this activity is that it gets you out of your head.

Sometimes if you can reverse your worries just a little, you can build up enough momentum to get you out of a tailspin and thinking in a positive direction—which will become its own fuel to get you flowing again.

This may be a good time for you to get more community: meet with friends for a little gab, and set up parties or conferences (if work-related).

Another way you can help quell worries is by increasing feedback you receive from others. Try meeting with a friend specifically for feedback.

Similarly, nurturing others who may need your help with their own worries can generate new perspectives to relieve your own.

∞ **Play music to help shift a mood.** Singing and chanting can brighten your moods. Try playing more music at various times during the day to boost your mood. Getting a drum, especially one you can hold in your hand and play it along with your favorite songs, is a great uplifting home activity that, historically, has been used to help synchronize many parts of the mind. Play seasonal songs. For extra effect, try singing along.

∞ **Take some time off.** This is an especially good time to take a personal day off at work. When you do, do so without expectation. Just enjoy. Try something seasonal.

∞ **Treat your fatigue.** You need to take care to manage sleep, physical activities, and nutrition to help prevent feeling fatigued as you transition into the falling energy of autumn. Fatigue can be brought on by physical and/or psychological reasons.

Ask:

* Am I getting enough physical activity?

* Am I getting enough sleep?

* How am I sleeping? Interrupted, uninterrupted? Insomnia?

* How has my diet been?

If your spirits are low, you can also feel fatigued.

Ask:

* Do I generally feel good? Optimistic? Alive? On purpose? Do I feel joy? Motivation? Direction? Boredom?

* Do I feel empty inside even though I am constantly achieving?

* Can I accept it when someone offers positivity or invites me into a positive experience?

* If not, what do I need to do to revitalize my spirits?

Note that if the mind is sick, the body can follow, and vice versa.

Frank is a senior citizen. He was recently involved in a car accident and incurred various physical injuries, including head trauma. He was hospitalized as a result and saw several physicians and specialists who, focused on his physical trauma, worked extensively with him toward recovery. Preliminary results came quickly and were good. At the end of one week, Frank was discharged. In the time that followed, the emotional effects of his accident, which had been overridden by the intensity of the physical problems, became more apparent. These seemed to grow out of various fears. Yet, it was during this time that he began putting pressure on himself (and others) to address some major life decisions he wanted to make. Much of this had to do with the fact that the accident had left him car-less, probably for good, and in need of rehabilitation.

Change—such as Frank's new reality sans vehicle—is hard to accept. This is why it is important to summon late summer's energy for some slow, gentle soul searching, and proceed from there. When you are hurt, healing must be allowed to occur, and the mind and body need time to properly re-stabilize. As much as Frank wanted to jump-start his healing process and get his life back together, he was in no shape to be making important life decisions under this emotional influence.

Instead of finding solutions, he felt more stress than ever. This caused him to rush back to his normal everyday activities without the benefits of rehabilitation. Frank's decision led to a fall which then added further restrictions to his life.

∾ **Mourn your losses.** When dealing with changes, you need an opportunity to mourn your losses. Frank could not just be *told* "Okay, now is the time for changes—you will no longer be driving your own car anymore even though you have for more than 60 years." He needed more time to stabilize his emotions and the thoughts they were provoking.

You cannot put this kind of pressure on yourself either. Sometimes we have to make changes gradually. Everyone needs time to be introspective, to mourn changes, to clearly see their new options, and reorganize. This process is healthy and necessary for transition.

෨ **Overcome the mourning of change.** Sometimes getting close to the environment helps with this. Try using its natural rhythms to soothe you as you attempt to envision new perspectives. Take a solo trip to a brook, river, waterfall, or ocean. Listen to the water's rhythms. Clear your mind and just put your attention on relaxing and listening. Don't resist your thoughts. This will only intensify them as well as your stress. Instead let them float through your mind fluidly, without sticking. See them float away. You may wish to make a recording of some of these sounds for later or purchase recordings of similar sounds. Note: Some people enjoy listening to white noise (which you can purchase on various locations online) to produce a similar effect at home. For our purposes, natural is best.

෨ **Ask for help.** Sometimes you just need feedback, especially during times of growth and even more so when that growth is in, for you, uncharted areas. Being around others can sometimes give you the energy boost and, importantly, the feedback you may need to find balance.

- ∾ **Deal with the neediness of others.** Be aware of others' neediness so that it doesn't boil up into conflict. Sometimes another's need for attachment, when unsatisfied, causes him or her to detach. Empathetic nurturing will help reverse this. You don't want your approach to be excessive (you may lose the ability to take care of your own matters) or deficient (you cannot contribute to the matter at hand), so balance is important. Sometimes calming another's fire during this season will bring you more of the peace and calm you need.

- ∾ **Improve memory.** Memory can be affected during this season. One explanation for this is that you are over-exerting yourself when you need to be calm. Another possibility is that you are feeling down and need a lift and so you don't have enough energy. Energy-calming or boosting techniques, as well as mood-shifting techniques, will help you regain this type of memory loss.

  Note: Avoid using caffeinated and energy drinks excessively.

- ∾ **Improve processing.** Meditate daily to slow yourself down or clear out blocks. Then, use music to stimulate yourself if you need more recharging.

- ∾ **Give.** Use your personal areas of abundance, expertise, and strength to help someone else achieve what you are trying to achieve. This energy will come back to you.

How to Cultivate the Spirit of Late Summer

A Late Summer Meditation

Each of the other seasons revolves around this season, which is at the center—your center, as well as the center of everything. Likewise, the late summer cycle radiates its influence into each of the others. When you are present to this movement, you put your Self into everything you do, and everything you do comes back and nurtures everything you are. You feel in sync and at peace with all of life.

Later summer is fertile ground. It is the mother of your being, from which you can be most nurturing and most practically creative. This is your mind's sweet spot, the hub of it all. This locus is the center of the universe within you and you within it. Centered, you are connected to who you are, want to be, and will be. You are home, within yourself and within all that exists. From here, you are able to make your dreams reality. This fertile ground is sacred.

Use this meditation daily:

Find a quiet place where you can relax. Close your eyes and breathe slowly, inhaling through your nose and exhaling through your mouth. Then focus your attention on your breath. Think of it as if you are breathing from the bottom of your lungs. Follow your breath down like an elevator to your abdomen. This is a major location of energy in your body. The Chinese refer to it as the lower *Dan Tien*, an area a few inches below your navel. This is also your body's exact center point of gravity. Visualize your energy as pure, white light. You can hold your hand to that part of your body so that you can create a target for your breath. Feel your energy surge with each in-breath. Feel your core strengthening. Outer strength comes from inner strength. Always focus on inner strength when you need to exert force.

Put your attention on your feet. With your eyes closed, try to feel the bottoms of your feet and the air surrounding them. Now the soles of your shoes and the floor beneath them. Move your attention to your legs, hips, waist, and the rest of your body—torso, shoulders, arms, hands—and back to your breath. With each in-breath, feel the energy coming into your body and mind from the crown of your head (this area is known as your upper Dan Tien) and up through your feet. Imagine each of these orbiting around your body simultaneously. Hold your hands as if holding a balloon in them, in front of your lower Dan Tien. Imagine the skin of the balloon suddenly disappearing. The energy that you feel welling up in between your hands is what's emanating from you and from the environment through you. Feel it surging. Feel this energy within yourself. Feel it flowing within the environment. Feel a part of it. Feel a part of it all.

Late Summer

Resolutions

- Today I try to live from center as much as possible.
- Today I will focus on how I transition from one situation to another. I will enter smoothly, exit smoothly—balanced—for entry into the next situation.

- ∞ Today I will take time to step back and pause. I will ask myself what part of me is growing in what I am doing.

- ∞ Today I will step back and pause. I will ask myself what part of others is growing in what they are doing.

- ∞ Today I will step back and pause. I will ask myself how what I (and others) do contributes to the growth of the world around us.

- ∞ Today I will identify one of my best talents and, at an appropriate time, let it flow into what I do.

- ∞ Today I will reflect on what triggers my irrational thoughts and actions. I will be aware; when I feel myself about to become irrational, I will reverse direction.

- ∞ Today I will pay attention to when I begin to detach from situations. I will take a breath and re-focus.

- ∞ Today I will look for the connection between things and parts of myself that I seeded in spring. I *will* use each to nourish and grow the other.

- ∞ Today I will compliment someone when I see him or her using a unique talent to benefit others.

AUTUMN

To see a world in a grain of sand
And heaven in a wild flower
Hold infinity in the palm of your hand
And eternity in an hour.
—William Blake

Falling Energy
Harvest
Letting Go
Abundance

Reflection
Assembly
Alternating Focus

Autumn begins in the Northern Hemisphere on September 22. Mornings open with a chill in the air and the crackle of dry leaves scattered on the ground. Afternoons are warm and, early in the season, they can still feel like summer—for a while. Depending on where you live, you can see some people walking around in shorts and others wearing sweaters and heftier coats, until the latter becomes the norm. Autumn nights get colder and deepen into a dark, crystal-clear, star-studded sky. The chill, in contrast to summer's heat, brings with it the smell of cider, wood smoke and bonfires, and many other seasonal scents.

Days begin their descent into darkness much earlier, and the nights get progressively colder, as will the mornings. There are predictably gray days. But these days are a good time to appreciate autumn colors as they flare under the gray skies.

Harvest

Autumn is the cycle for harvesting the good you have sown. It is also a time when many traditions give thanks and celebrate the abundance that you have reaped throughout the year.

Part of harvesting is identifying, among your new growth, the components that will nurture you and those that will not, at least presently. As the idiom goes, this is the time to "separate the wheat from the chaff." So autumn is also about gathering what you believe you will need, physically, mentally, and spiritually, as well as letting go of what is unnecessary, useless, or, perhaps, even harmful. Do keep this last detail in mind as it can be easy to overlook.

Your goal during the autumn cycle is dual: to take inventory and to also consciously prune. In order to do this effectively, you will need to keep a centered mind. This means tapping into the energy of late summer as well. This energy is your spotlight to illuminate what's working and what stays, and what must go.

Toggling between the currencies of late summer and autumn will help you avoid burning out and enable you to reel in what you believe really matters.

Melissa works for an organization that collects news and other information for the enrichment of business professionals and their staff. This September, Melissa and her husband had a second child. To help with the transition, she took off work until the beginning of November. When she returned, she planned to at least finish the year, which would take her to the end of December. As for "after that," she was undecided. She felt she wanted to make a change.

Melissa's return to work in November turned out to be difficult—physically—as she had to dig deep for the energy to tend to both her newborn and her job. She was running on reserves. Sure, she had "been there, done that" once before, but this time it was harder to get going again. She had changed. The job just didn't excite her the way it did when she had started.

She and her husband had carefully decided that returning and finishing off the year would be best. At worst, they thought, it would allow Melissa time to explore options.

Earlier this year, Melissa had put together an anti-bullying presentation for the local elementary school that her older son attended. The program was smart and dramatic and worked well with the children and, to her credit, with the teachers too. In fact, Melissa was invited back to give another presentation. Later, she was also invited to present the same program for the local Girl Scouts. By September, she had presented the workshop for several organizations, all with enthusiastic results.

Cresting on a wave, Melissa started a children's book over summer, on the subject of bullying. She really liked working on it as it combined her talent for writing and editing articles with her interest in children. She managed to publish an excerpt from the manuscript as an article in a parenting journal.

She made time to outline the rest of her book and began a list of potential publishers she thought might be interested in publishing it. She estimated that she could finish her book in about one year— if she could find a way to work on it full-time.

This would mean, however, leaving her 9-to-5 job, probably for good.

Her husband, after some discussion, encouraged her to follow her intuitions, saying his yearly raise could cover the need for more income.

When she closed her eyes, Melissa was able to see herself pursuing her dream.

ℭℛ

Melissa's younger sister, Jane, relocated this past year: first to New York City with her partner, where he had landed a job working for a large musical recording organization. She had similar credentials to his in recording, but he had gotten the job. While in New York City, she began spending long hours online, looking for potential recording work of her own that she could do from their small (but professional) home studio. She successfully contracted enough projects to make a salary and kept up searches for further employment, making more contacts—some coming, surprisingly, from the film industry.

When autumn arrived, instead of pursuing further recording projects at home, she made a demo of her work, including projects from past experience with film soundtracks. *Who knows?* she thought. *What if...*

What If?

Autumn is all about "what if" moments. Most of us have probably pondered "what if?" possibilities before. Maybe you have even discussed these potentials with your partner, family, and/or friends. Think about this: What if tomorrow you could do *whatever*—whatever you want? What if financial concerns were suddenly no factor at all? What would you do differently? I know this idea may sound impossible for most of us, but just roll with the possibility for a few minutes. Imagine: What would you do if you could just forget about finances? After all, it is just a thought!

The reason I am asking you to think about this is that this playful and simple thought will help give you more self-awareness and further definition in pursuing what is important in your life.

Melissa asked herself this question, and when she did, she realized that, at some deeper level, within that part of her that she didn't commonly share, she really would like to live differently. When she was honest with herself, she thought she would love giving presentations, and writing her children's book (and hopefully others) while raising her sons in an environment of closer contact. When she looked at the details of her life from her core, she saw this dream and path were suddenly realistically within her grasp.

For her sister, Jane, it was amazing to see what bubbled up in her "what if" moment as she slowed down enough to take a look at the details of her life as they had blossomed in the last few years. Once she relaxed and took a good, slow look, she started seeing how several pieces had suddenly unfolded. Now they were in close enough proximity to one another that she could see a very real possibility coming to life.

Both women asked *What if?* Both women felt the desire, motivation, and momentum for change. Both women would answer in their own way. But only one woman would follow her dreams.

Listen to the Message of Metal

Autumn is associated with the element of metal. Metal gives you the strength to resist things. It gives you the power of resolve. It is strong and consolidated, yet can turn liquid, becoming flexible when necessary. Metal can break things, break through things, hold things back, protect boundaries, clear paths for new endeavors, or widen an already existing path.

A metal person is resilient, clearheaded, focused, strong, knows herself, and is organized, methodical, and full of re-solve. She is willing to go where the going gets rough and often uncharted. She can set limits, lead, communicate, and work hard. She can stay on course. She can stave off unin-vited (or invited) distracters.

In the previous example, Melissa couldn't get her mind off financial matters. Her worries escalated into an imbal-anced attachment to autumn's metal element and created, within her, an impassible boundary to her own dream.

Jane, on the other hand, was able to tap into autumn's energy to carve a whole new path for herself, bringing to-gether the best of the new capabilities with pieces from her past. She had no idea when, where, or if further opportunity would come knocking, be she remained balanced, open, and flowing forward.

Watch Your Energy

During autumn, it is easy to feel stuck. Part of you may want to stick to the "old you" that, in some ways, has provided consistency in your life. As the season's energy begins a decline, it's easy to feel as though you don't want to tackle new additions to your life. This can leave you feeling aggressive about wanting to stick to the familiar comfort of regularity. The problem is that by sticking to old comfort zones, you may reject something new and potentially very good. By getting aggressive as natural energy declines you can tire even more.

For this reason, you need to closely consider what's on your plate and how it relates to your core dreams. Sometimes, everything on the plate looks good, but that doesn't absolutely mean that it *is* good for you. Similarly, everything you perceive as bad may not be bad for you either. So you need to look closely.

Ask yourself what you really want to "reel in" this autumn. Which new components do you want to nurture, invest more of yourself in, and grow further? When you feel most centered, do you see these components as genuinely part of who you are?

Unfortunately, in our previous story, Melissa began to fatigue under the responsibilities of her current employment and caring for her newborn. She did not step back and consider whether these influences were fogging up her otherwise heartfelt dream. Her thoughts then diverted from her dreams to worrying about not having enough money. Whenever she felt exhausted, she became even more fearful of her finances. She reasoned that she could think about change sometime later—when she had her energy and "mind" back.

Perceptions of Missed Opportunity

Missed opportunities can leave you feeling frustrated and unable to get your bearings. They can further your anxieties. This, in turn, can result in emotional swings. In such an instance, feelings of sadness can occur, and they can further develop into feelings of depression. It is not uncommon for one who has reached this state of depression to feel mentally paralyzed. This begins a troublesome swing amplified with both the feelings of fatigue and feelings of failure. Additionally, if you begin to feel you are stuck in a rut, you may start to think there is no way out. If you find that you cannot be at peace with a decision, it may be best to leave the door open to visit things later in time, as Melissa did when she chose to return to her long-time job.

Finding a Reference Point

A good way to turn feelings of missed opportunity around is to get a *reference point*—for example, identify someone who has successfully navigated through a similar situation. Perhaps your reference point is a former period or episode in your own life. Perhaps your reference point is a character from history or literature. The idea is to become aware of a solution through reference. Take your time finding what is closest to your situation and a procedure that is a good fit for you. Extract what is applicable to your situation and apply it.

Self-Awareness

The more self-awareness you maintain throughout this season of harvest, the better. In spring you seed a wide variety of possibilities. It is a time for you to flow your attention outward. In summer, you continue your outward attentions and connections and begin to nurture what you have seeded. In late summer, you turn your attention inward. You get in touch with your deeper Self and innermost dreams. In autumn you simultaneously look outward and inward, and see the matured fruit of your labor—grown now in abundance—as well as the seeds that simply never took root. It is up to you what you will harvest from all the growth.

Perhaps because of our efforts, perhaps because of the abundance and the sheer amount of growth we see (and for many other reasons), it is hard to decide among all our bounty which we will take in, further explore, invest in, organize, and create further in the months ahead. All this choice we have can weaken, distort, and even deteriorate our focus. It can spark dysfunctional feelings, particularly as your seasonal energy wanes.

You have to be careful because this pattern of negative feelings accompanied by a lack of focus can spiral out of control. This is why, again, it is so important to keep your emotions in check and peer both inside and outside yourself as you make these determinations. Looking at how the parts fit into and work with your "whole" person helps you decide.

The Difficulty of Letting Go

In the earlier examples of Melissa and Jane, although both women started out without apparent conflicts, Melissa's mind began to pull her in a direction controlled by her fears. Ultimately, this influence drove her back to an old path where she was less fearful, though less fulfilled, even though all of her support had pointed in the other direction. Melissa did not focus on those positive details, and instead was swept away by the mix of fatigue, fear, and need for comfort, and the downward spin those mechanisms created. Her mind headed down a path that took her further away from her dream. So she chose, in the end, to continue her old employment, and sacrificed her dream, for now.

On the other hand, her sister, Jane, became more excited by the possibilities she had generated. The more she slowed down, the more possibilities she saw, the more excited she got. Her mind headed down a path that would bring her closer to her dream, so she followed it with vigor.

Why is it that some individuals have difficulty letting go of things? One reason is that the consequences of some decisions/behaviors are not immediate; that is, they arrive further down the line. This is the problem many times with addictions, such as those of food, alcohol, smoking, relationships, work, and so on. Because we can so easily think that "one more time" won't hurt anything, when significant consequences don't look immediate, we allow ourselves to keep doing what we are doing, even if what we are doing isn't healthy. Sometimes if we see that other people are engaged in similar dysfunctional behavior, we can justify our own.

Sometimes, certain thoughts, feelings, and actions have been imbedded in you for years via your culture (work, family, geographic location, and so on). As such, these become more resistant to change. Sometimes the value of behaviors is gauged by their obvious feel-good immediacy. So, as with Melissa, the challenge is to get ourselves to see the rewards of longer-range, subtler options, especially when they offer a potentially greater advantage.

The following is a self-scan that can help you with such decisions:

- **Ask:** What is the true contribution of new developments that I see manifesting in my life? Am I influenced by any false information regarding them? Am I placing any false value on these developments?

- **Ask:** What could I actually do with these new components? What do I wish to do with them? What should I do with them?

- **Action:** Step back. Gather credible, accurate information to help you decide.

- **Take charge:** Make your decision.

- **Action:** Reward yourself for (A) Finding and locating helpful and good information, and (B) for then doing what is best for you.

Sadness

Sadness and grieving can manifest as an imbalance in autumn. Yes, they are an essential part of letting go, but they can also block your mind, social life, work life, and home life with doubt. This can begin a downward cycle that gets bigger and harder to control. So it is important to try to recognize your sadness and doubt.

For some people, this is painful. The easiest thing for these individuals to do to quell the sadness is simply deny it exists. This reaction uses the autumn element of metal in a dysfunctional way, forming a barrier to the truth so as to avoid having to deal with it. It abdicates the stewardship of your own mind to someone (or some "thing") else.

Increase Your Psychological Currency

Increasing your psychological currency—the psychic energy and information you need (cognitive and emotional) to keep you feeling positive and flowing—is a good idea during nature's falling energy cycles. This will help you stay balanced, see solutions more clearly, and deal with the residuals of letting go of items you nurtured and grew that are just not fitting into your life now. It will help you, as William James says, to keep possession of your mind.

The following exercise can help you put some good, energizing information in your pocket if you are experiencing any doubt regarding decisions you've made during this cycle. You may, at the end of the day, find that you can reaffirm your decision, and therefore letting go becomes easier. Or you may decide it's all worth another look.

- **Ask:** What is the source of my doubt?
- **Ask:** What personal filters am I putting on the situation I want changed?
- **Ask:** Are any of these filters being driven by my sadness?

- જી **Ask:** What cultural filters am I putting on to justify inaction?

- જી **Ask:** Are any of these filters being driven by my sadness?

- જી **Ask:** Why is my culture telling me I should feel sad?

- જી **Action:** Challenge these filters.

- જી **Ask:** Is this true or not? Is this reasonable, especially in my specific case? Is this authentic to my specific case and thinking? Am I being swayed because others are doing thusly? How is their situation like my own? Unlike? What are the immediate and long-range benefits or liabilities of such thinking in my life? To others?

- જી **Ask:** How is my sadness affecting my daily goals? Did I greet one person one way and another differently today? What does this tell me about how sadness can affect me?

Note: The way out of this conflict is to make a decision to release it. Feel your sadness. Challenge it. Take action.

Getting your mind flowing during nature's falling energies doesn't have to be a monumental effort. Sometimes little efforts are just as good. But it is important that you do so because you can have the benefits of this great mindset as your own energies wane throughout each day.

Years ago I used to watch my *sensei* sweeping the floor of the dojo before classes. Sometimes he would do this for half an hour. I learned a lesson in humility watching him do this, but I also learned how easy it can be to organize the mind. One day, I noticed how focused he was as he swept. Not focused as though he was burning holes into the floor with his eyes, looking for every little particle of debris left there, but more as though his eyes were wide pools of water reflecting the entire sky.

When I went home that night, I tried it myself. I was amazed to discover just how comforting such a simple task could be. The more I got into it, the more I flowed with it, and the more de-stressed I felt. Not only that, but afterward, my mind felt activated, organized, and calm.

What an easy way to stop spinning your wheels in the muck and get yourself to higher ground, I thought. To this day, this is one of my favorite methods for getting my mind relaxed, alert, and organized. In autumn, I also enjoy raking leaves—different package, but same effect.

Find a basic activity that works for you, and do it often.

Optimizing Autumn Energy

Autumn offers us a variety of tools to sustain our good energy and also build more as nature's energy begins its decline.

Because you are still in close proximity to summer's high rising energy and still caught up in it, you may yet feel the effect of fired-up motivations and outreaches. You may, as many do, still feel like circulating, growing, and bringing these ambitions to fruition.

But autumn provides the necessary decline of energy we all need to take a slower and closer look at the way things we have seeded and blossomed turned out. Now is your time to harvest them, organize them, and put up your protective boundaries to help them endure. Autumn is your time to leave any dysfunctional growth at the door.

To optimize your activities, seek tranquility this season and preserve your energy. Spend time centering and exploring more about who you are, what you have, and what you need—and especially how this can all fit together. Spend time outside to experience the seasonal patterns of slowing down: from cool and less light, to warm and more light, to cooler and earlier dark. Let these patterns sink into your mind. Use them to energize your own activities and to stay in balance.

Debbie says she has to get a prescription for antibiotics nearly every year in mid-autumn. This is because she has to deal with the same infection every year at this time. Sometimes, she says, it escalates to bronchitis.

This year, however, Debbie was able to ward off the infection all together. One of the things she attributes this to is her coming to the realization that during autumn her energy tends to frenzy. This is because, ironically, she doesn't have enough energy when she needs it. Her lack of energy influences her ability to focus efficiently and to get organized. These elements lower her mood and then she gets even less done, she says, which increases her anxieties and eats away more energy. The next thing you know, she says, she is having trouble sleeping. It's like a snowball that keeps getting bigger. Then, she starts feeling sick with muscle pains, headaches, sore throats, and flu-like symptoms.

So what did she do differently this year? (1) She maintained a regular exercise regimen as autumn progressed, something she usually tends to cut out almost completely until after the holidays. This kept her overall energy and focus up. (2) She got more sleep by going to bed earlier. (3) She ate moderately, avoiding the urge to overeat, especially as the holidays approached. As part of her diet, she treated herself to a cup of white tea after dinner, which she believed aided digestion and bumped up her metabolism in the evening. (4) She reflected on new facets of her life that she had grown throughout the year and made sure she had time to start piecing them together into a bigger and stronger picture. She also got rid of anything that didn't fit her current life trajectory. (5) She looked for the positive in every day.

She did begin to feel the first tug of sickness by early November, but this year she was able to ward it off. By identifying issues she believed contributed to her yearly autumn illness, she was able to write her own prescription to reverse them.

Exercises

ꙮ **Practice empty mind.** If something in your life has you down, trying to look toward the positive can help. Try these two Zen techniques: First, use the concept of *Mushin* (Japanese for "empty mind"). To practice Mushin, empty your mind of all negative emotions. This enables you to be more present and get your mind flowing again. Then, add to that the Zen concept of *Beginner's Mind*. This mindset carries within it no preconceived ideas. It attempts to see things as they are. Therefore you are open to all possibilities. Beginner's Mind is like a bowl of clear, vibrant attention. Pure and alert, this is the awareness with which we are born.

ꙮ **Exercise (with moderation) to build energy.** Start in the morning if you can. This will get your energy moving throughout the whole day. Then, as if you were taking medication, introduce a second dose of exercise (moderate) in your afternoon if possible, around when your daytime energies start to wane. Moderate exercise will help keep you focused and give you the psychic energy you need for the rest of your day and evening. The best policy is to remember to keep all things in moderation.

ꙮ **Add something new to spice up your exercise.** You'll need it. This season may be the time to start something different to excite your motivation. This can be in the form of a new jogging (or walking) route or a new program such as rock climbing, hiking, yoga, martial arts, or racquetball. Try adding a new piece of equipment, a "toy" so to speak, to your current exercise program. Do this before the long stretch of shorter daylight arrives. Sometimes new gear or a new apparatus is all you need to get motivated again. It can be as simple as a new outfit or sneakers, or even a new playlist on your iPod. This will be a good way for you to prepare to ward off lower-energy moods and days when they hit. You will have a built-in prescription to reverse them.

     ⅎ **Optimize your sleep.** Get to bed earlier; you need a bit more sleep to balance this cycle's falling energy. Use music and mediation to help lull you into sleep and also to help you attain deeper and more satisfying rest.

    If you are using music, remember you can create your own personal lullaby. Songs from your childhood work very well. Do you know any tunes that you and your mom used to listen to together or that your mom used to listen to? Psychologically there is a genetic connection between you and your parents, particularly your mom, in terms of disposition. So if you have a close relationship with your mother this is a good opportunity to explore some of the songs she was listening to before you were born, even before you were conceived. What worked to relax her brain can work on you! If a specific musical piece made her feel calm or happy or excited, it can have a similar effect on you.

Bear in mind that, generally, songs with a BPM (beats per minute) under 100 are a good place to start looking. But don't let that stop you from using a slightly higher BPM. If the song relaxes you because of soothing memories and/or feelings you have attached to it, then by all means add it to your iPod and use it.

ɕɔ **Absorb autumn's colors.** Spend some time outdoors just taking in autumn's colors. Fill your eyes and mind with them. Make yourself aware of how observing them makes you feel mentally and physically—which landscapes relax your mind and body, and which can you feel uplifting you? Commit these images and the feelings associated with them to memory. Visualize them throughout the day when you can benefit from that certain type of energy. Take some pictures and create a short slide show on your cell phone or other electronic device. This way you can just push the *Play* button whenever you need it.

ɕɔ **Organize.** An easy way to organize during this cycle is to clean up the clutter around your living environment. Just as in our earlier example of sweeping floors, cleaning up the clutter in your living space will revitalize your mind's sense of organization and bring you some clean, stress-free energy and a sense of reward. Take your time as you do this; slow down, calm your breathing, and put your whole focus on the task. You may like to augment your housework with soft, soothing music. Do you have any music your parents used to listen to when you were a child and they were engaged in housework? Or better yet, when you were helping them with chores? These songs work beautifully.

Try organizing in the evening. You may find that you will get a better night's sleep and wake up feeling more organized. Working with your hands is a great stress-buster and a good way to improve and preserve memory functions.

∾ **Do a self-scan.** Regularly take some time to review what attitudes and patterns have emerged in your life that need to be better synchronized with your goals. Then, strategize ways to harmonize beneficial patterns and eliminate any that will impede goals. Focus on how these negative patterns can be replaced with more positive behaviors that are more in sync with your goals. Until you have eliminated these patterns, reward yourself for just having begun to strategize a solution.

∾ **Pay special attention to your breathing.** Autumn energy is associated with the lungs. Think about it: it's a notorious season for sinus infections, colds, and the flu. Stop what you are doing now and then and check how you are breathing—predictably, your breaths will be shallow. Simply adjust and breathe deeper and slower—whatever is comfortable for you. Use your measured and abdominal breathing techniques. Little by little, you can train yourself to breathe more deeply and more relaxed.

∾ **Discover your internal warmth again.** Whereas external heat can—in excess—take your energy away, internal heat—not in excess—can help fuel your energy. It will loosen you up and motivate you. But don't get too aggressive in staving off the cold. Use it to help your mind and body move into the season at a slower, clearer, and more balanced pace. If the cold starts to bog you down, locate your inner warmth and circulate it to get you going again.

ဢ **Try not to take on any (major) new work.** Taking on new projects can shift your focus away from where it needs to be: on harvesting and organizing your bounty—without which you can forfeit many of the benefits that will come with all you have gained. De-focusing now could result in missing necessary information on how it all fits, as well as what else may be needed to keep moving things forward and growing them. Stay focused on assembling the pieces of your bounty. Do, however, allow some new tasks to enter your routines if they are necessary for achieving this assembly.

ဢ **Be social and accept the congeniality and hospitality of others.** The upcoming holidays are pre-made to help out with this objective. You can use get-togethers to help relax, reduce stress, and get you sorting things out. Socializing also gives you the opportunity to help others with their needs.

ဢ **Use a lot of reflection.** Because this is the cycle of harvesting all you have sown, make daily time for reflection. See the abundance. See it from your center. See it clearly. Evenings and nights, when your energy is waning (but you are not yet too mellow) work best.

Recently I was planning on making a shift in my own career. The shift was into private practice, involving full-time writing, research, and consulting. This was a big change for me, but it had been in my heart for a long time, so I was really excited to make it happen. Feeling the need for change and then seeing how new growth in my life could foster it is what set this new phase of my career in motion.

ॐ **Pay attention to nutrition.** Use more warming (cooked) foods during this season, such as soups, stews, and steamed vegetables, as well as more meats, beans, and nuts. Add squashes, leeks, sweet potatoes, and onions to your list. Watch out for excessive use of richer foods. Over-eating and cravings can kick in during this cycle, especially with the combination of waning energy and holiday festivities. Lemon and water, particularly warm, will help curb your appetite. You can try this drink before meals and it will help balance your appetite. Try adding a little natural sweetness such as honey or syrups and your warm lemon drink will put a little oomph into your morning startup. White, green, chai, and ginger teas are often good complements to keeping your diet and metabolism in check and also providing that extra, yet balanced energy boost you may need.

Correcting Autumn Imbalances

As nature's energy dips and you are faced with the chores of gathering, amassing, and storing, it is easy to get into the imbalance of overdoing things. Likewise, it is easy to start minimizing, at times, important things, especially if you don't have the energy to meet these challenges. Leaving important issues unaddressed can land you in negative moods that, in turn, can further inhibit your activity and decision-making ability. Tiredness and anxiety are both tip-offs of imbalance this season.

When you are low in energy, you can also feel low in inspiration. This makes it difficult to know how or even whether you should wrap your arms around what you and life have blossomed or whether you are better off clipping some things off your to-do list.

This, then, is where the element of metal, if imbalanced, can become problematic, blocking your ability to make such decisions. If that happens, especially in situations in which you need a more adaptable and inspired mindset, you may end up with issues such as (1) the inability to move forward with an idea or situation that is good, and (2) feelings of inflexibility, detachment, deteriorating self-awareness, depression, interpersonal difficulties, and physical illness.

Some indicators that your energy may be running out of sync this season include experiencing respiratory problems, ranging from sinus to bronchial; low energy; dehydration; intestinal disorders; downward mood swings; excessive grief; compulsiveness; and difficulty keeping or accepting boundaries. If you are feeling any of these things you may be out of balance with this season's energy. Luckily, the autumn cycle offers a wide variety of ways to find your balance.

Garret has had a good year in terms of work, health, and recreational activity. He enjoyed socializing with his friends, but has not seen them much lately. Life, as Garret put it, had slammed a one-two punch into his otherwise good year. First, there was the troublesome and painful breakup with his fiancée, with whom he had partnered for five years. Then there was the sudden death of his dog, a Labrador retriever, whom he'd had in his life for two years.

The combination of these two events left Garret feeling down. He'd stopped wanting to see anyone. The shortened daylight of autumn as well as the coming holiday season seemed to worsen his mood. He was losing interest in many of the things he loved, such as athletics, socializing, and weekend pleasure trips. He was also losing his competitive edge at work and felt like he was floundering.

He felt uninspired and often not just low on energy, but physically weak too. Looking down autumn's long and darkening road, Garret didn't see any comforting light ahead.

He realized in many ways his own energy was mismatched with the environment. Instead of abundance, he felt only absence.

One of the first indicators, to him, was the way he'd been talking lately. He thought of himself as upbeat, but there wasn't anything upbeat coming out of his mouth. As his mood sunk so had his words.

He didn't feel attentive lately. He noticed this most when he was driving and his mind wandered. He often felt sad and wondered what it would take to get him up and going again.

∞ **Reverse worries.** It is common, during this season when energies begin their decline, to become worried about your future. Some individuals express this worry in the inability to let go of certain facets of their life, including feelings that have become damaging. Others become compulsively driven to certain goals, to the detriment of the other goals. These actions disturb your flow of positive energy. As with the other emotions, you have to keep worries in check. They will drain you if you don't. They will impede your focus. You need time to recharge and clear out your mind to control your worries. You also need time to replenish your body with the nutrients and rest it needs to keep you both focused and healthy. Start by using autumn's coolness to help you cool down. Find this energy inside you or go outside, but either way, connect with fall's cooling, declining energy. Use some mild physical exercise. Tai Chi, Yoga, and Chi Kung are good for de-stressing and widening your focus again. Stretch. Breathe. Re-charge.

🔊 **Later, let go of your worries.** Once you are re-charged, step back and ask yourself what's going on, with the objective of letting go.

* **Ask:** Are my feelings of worry evolving from internal or external aspects of my life?

* **Ask:** What are these aspects? Are they reasonable, accurate assessments? How are my feelings influencing my ability to deal with these elements?

* **Ask:** How significantly are my feelings affecting my goals? Are these core goals?

* **Ask:** How have similar worries affected me in the past? Do I need to change that? What part?

* **Ask:** What lifestyle changes can I make to help stave off my ruminations?

* **Ask:** What lifestyle changes can I make to help scaffold a plan to resolve these ruminations?

* **Action:** Start making these changes and reward yourself for having started.

* **Action:** Continue physical exercise to drain off negative energy and replenish good energy.

🔊 **Broaden your focus.** Be careful not to hold too tight a focus even on a good idea or you may dry it up. Physical dryness is part of this season, but it can manifest as psychological dryness as well. The idea is not to put all your eggs in one basket, as the saying goes. Consider this adage in terms of nutrition, daily responsibilities, thoughts, and feelings. As you review your harvest, keep a wide lens.

∮ **Deal with sadness and grief.** Try beginning with some moderate exercise—just enough to empty some of the negative energy (if not all) and replace it with clean, higher, more positive energy. Then, once you've shifted your energy, try meditating. Go inward. Soul-search. Then, go outward. See what you can organize from the good that has recently entered your life. Use this to aim at achieving a reachable goal: Small and basic may be best. Then repeat and keep repeating this process daily. Keep it light, especially at first. It may take a while to see results, but when you do, keep going with the process of setting small goals until you can get back to regular activities in a more positive mindset.

If you can't seem to turn it around, make yourself more aware.

✱ **Ask:** What do I do well when I am sad?

✱ **Action:** Immerse yourself in activities that you do well when sad.

Or, don't devote so much energy to certain perceptions.

✱ **Tell yourself:** Things can and will change even if it takes a week or more.

✱ **Tell yourself:** I will let myself feel down—for a while. (Give yourself a reference, say, a week. Then, review things again.)

If you need to, make use of your interpersonal support system. Or you may need to seek professional care.

ᔥ **Reverse loneliness.** Join a sport or social group in your community or neighborhood. You can also try doing some volunteer work; you can use a skill you have developed to help others. You can also do much-needed work such as volunteer at a soup kitchen, hospice, library, or senior center. This will leave you feeling good about yourself. Then that feeling of goodness and reward will snowball. Tap into your creative brain. Try painting or playing music or creative writing.

   If you can't seem to turn it around, make yourself more aware.

   ✳ **Ask:** What do I do well when I am lonely?

   ✳ **Action:** Immerse yourself in activities that you do well when lonely.

ᔥ **Be aware of harmful feel-good compulsions.** As energy declines, still high off of summer's soaring energy, autumn's energy can seem even lower, and some individuals' pleasure-seeking circuits go awry and start hunting pleasure wherever they can get it. Take control of feel-good compulsions such as overeating, drinking alcohol, and spending. A gentle reminder of this tendency can prevent you from chasing some risky rewards and better manage signs of lower motivation.

ᔥ **Reverse weakening memory.** First, see what's going on.

   ✳ **Ask:** What is impeding my ability to recall?

✻ **Ask:** Am I too inundated with information and can't focus on all of it? Am I too tired to identify and focus on things?

✻ **Ask:** Am I over-stimulated due to pressures, stresses, or emotions (fear of failure, perfectionism, and so on)?

✻ **Ask:** Am I under the influence of emotions that are depleting my energy?

✻ **Ask:** Is it a matter of organization?

✻ **Ask:** What do I have in my toolbox to turn these conditions around?

✻ **Action:** Use your seasonal tools to reverse these conditions.

✻ **Then ask:** Do I need anything else to help me deal with the identified problems? How can I acquire these tools?

✻ **Action:** Use music. Create a musical anchor. First decide whether you need to go up or down. Then choose the music that you already think will do that for you. Holiday music is great to treat memory during this time of year. Also keep in mind that you can create new musical memories during this season so that you will have a good functional prescription afterward.

✻ **Action:** Increase exercise programs.

✻ **Action:** Visualize yourself doing something athletic. Breathe slower and deeper. Put a red lens over the whole visual. Breathe that picture in.

  Reverse guilt. Guilt may arise during this season if you feel your bounty is not abundant enough. Take a close look at what has come your way recently (if nothing comes to mind, you may need to pick an earlier starting date for "recently"). See how you can scaffold elements of your life toward reaching new and different goals. Identify a variety of sources where you can find information to help you with organization and planning. These may include experts who have written in your area of interest, friends, classes, and so on. Start building your scaffold.

How to Cultivate the Spirit of Autumn

An Autumn Meditation

After a brisk walk or just having spent some time outdoors, find a quiet place. Sit. Take a few slow, relaxing breaths. Imagine the cider-scented breeze and crisp leaves whisking across the ground. Let their colors float across your mind as if across a still and glowing lake. Memorize the autumn flowers ripe with their reds, yellows, purples, blues, and whites, perfuming the acres of golden light pouring onto the grasses and hillsides and gilding the mountaintops. Breathe in slowly, noticing the scent of pine cones and sap in the cool air. Breathe in even more slowly, and let a scene you composite from your distant past, from your happiest, most comforting autumns of childhood, play in your mind. Play it out like a scene from an old movie you love. See yourself in this scene interacting with your friends or family. Feel the safety and comfort arise again within you now. When you inhale,

inhale this whole picture into your body and mind. Let it flow through you, bringing its comfort everywhere. Let it soothe those parts of you where you feel tightness or pain. Flow with this scene for a while. Feel its warmth radiating within your solar plexus. Feel it radiating throughout you, then outward into the entire environment. Feel the web of energy that is you, your body, your mind, and your environment. Feel the inseparability of this connection. Just feel it as one continuous flowing. Relax; slow down. Let images of goodness that grew from this year's seasons float across your mind. Invite the ones that have been under your radar to stay a while longer, but don't disturb them; just watch. Gently ask yourself, *What do I need to gather?* Don't have a conversation with yourself; just see the response in images. Don't question these images, but do allow yourself to have feelings about them. Pay attention to, but don't question or stick to, any of your feelings. Just let them bubble up into your consciousness and float through you. Gently ask, *If money were of no issue, how would I organize my gifts of goodness into my life?* Don't respond with words. See your answer in images or pictures. Let these sink into your mind and circulate throughout your body. Feel them. Gently ask yourself, *What aspects of recent growth in my life are unnecessary?* Again, don't answer. Just see your answer in calm images. Acknowledge them. Take a slow, deep breath, and release these images. Watch them float out of your mind. Go back to your desired image of change in your life. See the goodness of the gifts that you have accrued that will now help get you there. Let this picture sink into your memory. Take a slow, deep breath. Center the picture in your solar plexus. See it filling with autumn's golden light. When you exhale, radiate this image into your environment. Take a moment and give thanks.

Resolutions

Autumn

- ✂ Today I will try to stop some of the chatter that goes on in my mind as I simply try to be present.

- ✂ Today I will randomly make myself aware of my thoughts and feelings and identify negative activity and why it's occurring, as well as positive thoughts and feelings and why they are present. I will use what I discover to better shift from negative to positive and to bring on more positive mindsets.

- ✂ Today I will identify what is detrimental to my greater goals.

- ✂ Today I will try to delete negative habits.

- ✂ Today I will begin to let go of dysfunctional elements in my life.

- ✂ Today I will make myself aware of negative language I use.

- ✂ Today I will try to eliminate negative language.

- ✂ Today I will identify any things that are making me sad.

- ✂ Today I will reflect on internal and external tools I have that can work to reverse my sadness.

- ✂ Today I will empty my cup and make way for the new.

- ✂ Today I will make a conscious effort to do something kind without expectation of return.

- ✂ Today I will dance.

WINTER

After a still winter night I awoke with the impression that some question had been put to me, which I had been endeavoring in vain to answer in my sleep, as what—how—when—where? But there was dawning Nature, in whom all creatures live, looking in at my broad windows with serene and satisfied face, and no question on her lips. I awoke to an answered question, to Nature and Daylight.

—Henry David Thoreau

Falling Energy
Calm
Creativity
Storage
Flow
Inspiration
Pure Potential

The energy of winter is mystical in many ways. As in the Thoreau quote (page 173), it is the energy of deep discovery.

Winter is the season for rest, reflection, and conservation of your physical and psychic energies, of finding safety and creativity in the bare energy of life—nature's and your own. The winter cycle is your body, mind, and spirit's restart button. With it you flow into that part of your mind that houses profound insights as you prepare to "reboot" into the new spring ahead and begin nature's cycles again.

Winter begins on December 21 (or sometimes the 22). This day is usually associated with the winter solstice, what we refer to as the shortest day of the year—or the longest night.

As autumn segues into the winter, nature enters a period of continued falling energy and rest. There is less sunlight now, temperatures get cold, and you naturally feel like slowing down your life and nourishing yourself on warmer, wholesome foods. The plush foliage and colors of summer and autumn are diminished now and in many cases are husked down to the simplest essentials of the landscape as nature dips way down into the zero point of its core where the energy of restoration and creation resides.

Within this cycle, you will experience pure creativity, and your capacity to create balance, profound satisfaction, and deep success is infinite and boundless. This is the place from which you can forever renew and generate not just your energy, but also yourself—and your life.

To this end, holistic arts suggest that the winter season is mostly a time of calm creation. It is your opportunity to get in touch with your life's dreams, to embrace and enjoy your life's mystery, and creatively assemble all that you have cultivated. This is your cycle to take a slower look to see the deeper wisdom and potential in what you have grown and gathered throughout the year. Winter is the time and energy to begin to creatively assemble this wisdom and potential into an assortment of little energy bundles that will act like the DNA of your dreams come springtime.

Picture this: A woman (or man) awakens in a small—actually, tiny—mountain town in upstate New York that has mostly been built up around a mid-sized mountain lake. The majority of the area is lightly forested, and the gunmetal light of December spreads a steely sheen on everything. It has snowed early this season, and there are about three inches of old snow and ice on the ground, plus a few squatty snow banks. It is an especially cold morning. The woman dresses in sweats and a warm woolen hat and heads out for an early morning jog. A light rain misted the trees and power lines overnight, and when the rain ended, everything went into a deep freeze. Now all is glistening as if everything were made of crystal. *It's magical*, she thinks. **And when she has this thought, something warms inside her. When she feels this, she thinks there is something mysterious that occurs in such environments and moments. This mystery, she is beginning to believe, has a profound effect on her.**

She remembers a line from the iconic writer Virginia Woolf about such experiences. Woolf referred to them as "moments of being." Right now she feels just as Woolf described: content, in sync with something bigger—perhaps the greater good. She feels in touch with herself. She feels alive, and puts her attention to herself feeling alive. According to the various holistic arts she practices, the cold makes it easy to locate Self, and the more you try, she has come to learn and realize, the stronger and tighter you can focus.

She remembers a line from a book she once read by the philosopher Alan W. Watts. She recalls his explanation of an Eastern concept that suggests how somewhere inside the feeling of cold you can locate a feeling of warmth, and vice versa. She has found that place inside herself. And now a rewarding wave of goodness spreads through her.

She walks briskly for about an eighth of a mile, as is her habit. She tries a technique she learned in a breathing lesson years earlier. She breathes in through her nose to the count of 1-2-3-4. Then she exhales to the same count. She puts her focus on the whooshing sound of her breath. This empties her mind of all but the feeling of goodness and warmth inside.

She loses any sense of time and falls into the rhythm and sound of her breathing. Then she breaks into a light jog. It begins snowing thickly. Flakes cling to her eyelashes. She doesn't know how long this has been occurring, yet when she becomes aware of it, she squints and peeks through her icy lashes to enjoy how they have prismed the light.

She notices too how the chill (which doesn't feel chilly to her anymore) has helped rid her of stressors. She makes a mental note of that.

She can feel that her focus has lightened, also thanks to the cold. She is confident that, if she wanted to, she could intensely focus on anything, yet her mind would remain light, supple, flexible, and quick. She has entered what could be defined as a state of flow. And this feeling is one of the main reasons she jogs every other day throughout winter.

She also likes that she can sustain her flowing mindset into things she wants to do even late into the day—sometimes even into the next day. And she is getting better at turning on the effect at will whenever she needs it, without the jog—even in other seasons. It's like a mental file she can access whenever she wants. All she needs to do is take a few measured breaths. The rhythmic sound of her breathing combined with the recollection of a few images of her jog is all she needs to trigger the feeling whenever she needs it.

She won't go so far as to describe herself as a winter person all the time, but she *has* discovered what winter's energies (in her internal and external environments) are good for and has learned to use them well.

Listen to the Message of Water

Winter, as it is to our mountain jogger, is all about entering and sustaining flow. It may seem a little strange at first, but the cold helps you find the warmth inside. So you want to make a mental map of what it feels like. It works as a "cool" inhibitor of distractions. It can very quickly snap you away from things that are dysfunctional and perhaps damaging to you and re-focus you on what is really important. You don't, however, have to be involved in athletics to experience this kind of psychological flow and focus—although athletic activities are a good way in.

In Eastern traditions, winter is associated with the element of water, which itself facilitates focus. Water can be soft or hard, still or moving, and can flow over, under, or even through things. It can float things or float atop things. It can absorb. It is formless and can adapt to any container. It can vaporize or become invisible. Whenever you feel apprehensive about where you are, especially during winter, the season of water, ask yourself: *Which characteristic of water should I apply in this situation?* Water is your guide post. If you need perspective on how to enhance a specific feeling or circumstance, imagine: Which characteristic of water would best apply?

Water—as is winter—is the symbol of purity, birth, and rebirth. When you embody the characteristics and influence of this life-giving force you are going with the flow. You fill each moment with inspired living; you force nothing; you become, you experience, and you interrelate.

During the winter cycle, a very special characteristic of water is emphasized. Flowing toward the path of least resistance, water can guide you into the calmest yet most powerful creative waters of your Self. Here is where you will formulate and store your little energy bundles that will surge from you with strength, purpose, and re-creation in the spring.

Using winter's energy to flow inward and take a good, slow look makes sense. From this deep well, you can create a future of your deepest desires.

How to Go With the Flow

Getting into and sustaining a flowing mind is a hallmark of living with each of the seasons. And it is at the heart of the winter cycle.

The winter mind does not think so much in what we call *top-down processing* or choosing to do something simply because this is what is expected of you or this is how such and such is "always" done. The winter mind is too creative for that. It places you in the emerging present, participating with all that flows.

For many of us, this is an entirely different way of thinking and responding to life. It can be, however, very quickly freeing. And because the freedom to allow life to emerge and to allow ourselves to engage with it are not just essentials of winter, this core influence of winter energy can and should be applied year-round, as well as in your day-by-day, moment-by-moment activities. Train your mind to use this energy during the full extent of winter. This constant training is what allows your mind to begin to automatically go there when it needs to during the rest of the year!

Flow Away from Your Stress

Stress comes from conflict. During the winter season, predictable conflicts are so big you can't miss them. The good thing is that this helps you get prepared and head your stress off at the pass.

When going with winter's flow—that is, in synchronizing with it—you will not feel stuck when the environment around you slows down and you are naturally beginning to decelerate yourself. In fact, you will be able to slow down with it. It is no accident that you are starting to crave a little more warmth and introspection. In doing so, you are in line with seasonal influences. The problem is that many individuals begin to feel the strain that can accompany this season—and for some people this gets to the point of majorly stressing out. What drives this stress is the attempt to keep up with the challenges of work, interpersonal relationships, holidays, and typical daily routines, most of which do not typically slow down and are probably out of whack with the environment's falling energies—and yours!

Synchronizing with "them" instead of nature's calming energy will take a toll on you. Typically your world of obligations pushes forward regardless of you and your natural environment, making what you feel are unreasonable demands. At worst, if you ignore this imbalance with nature, you enable the dysfunction to continue. At best, you recognize it and take charge to rebalance yourself and your responses to it. In the latter, you can make a positive difference in your own life, and, perhaps, in the lives of others around you.

Enter the mind of winter. Be like water. Go with the flow; rather than interfering with action, become part of it, allowing things to go their natural course. Be like the mirrored surface of undisturbed water—keep your mind still and awake, softly reflecting everything, lovely or dreadful, without allowing anything to get stuck. Be soft on the outside and strong on the inside. Be fully aware. Be slow, observe, take note, be introspective, and ponder. Respond in tranquility. Respond in peace.

The Last Deed

If you were able to husk your essence down to its smallest possible particle or blow it up to its largest, you would be at the point of pure, creative potential. What gets in the way of your creative power is the plethora of information that your mind downloads from birth onward—much of this operating unconsciously. This idea takes us back to Chapter 1, where we spoke of how information invades your mind uninvited from the moment you are born. Then, later, like a computer virus, this information dictates how your mind operates. Harmful images in your mind you have of yourself and the world want to run your life and you begin to believe that these images are who you really are, that the world is really this way, and you start using your energy as well as nature's energy to sustain this image.

Mythologist Joseph Campbell called these restrictions on your mind the *ego*. Ego, for Campbell, is the force that is holding us back. According to Campbell, in his book *The Power of Myth*, ego is "what you think you want, what you will to believe, what you think you can afford, what you decide to love, what you regard yourself bound to."

Then he went on to say, "It may all be too small, in which case it will nail you down.... Ultimately the last deed [letting go of the ego] must be done by you." You want to dissolve ego because, as Campbell explains, it is a main source of inaccurate reads of one's best potentialities. But why and how do you do that?

Centering the mind keeps the ego from nailing you down. This is because the centered mind is balanced, stable, and, simply speaking, *you*. It is able to access, comprehend, and orchestrate your mind-body-spirit. When you move forward from there, you move naturally. And the more you practice, the better you get at it.

It is the winter cycle and the winter mind that are able to muster the right energy to put, if you will, the "big chill" on stressors that arise from the conflict between your ego and who "you" really are and re-channel your energy to where it will do you the most good.

The winter person is able to freeze what is pushing her in an unsatisfactory direction, and step back. She will pause and ultimately liberate herself. She will center her visions and thoughts and feel at peace and free to create the life she wants. She will let this vision flow from her core and extend to her life and environment.

The winter mind is aware, spontaneous, and intelligent. It is limitless, and, as such, cannot be *nailed down* as long as you maintain it.

A winter person is egoless, natural, and ever-changing.

Creativity Rules

Once you remove the ego, creativity makes sense. This is because creativity must come from what you see, think, feel, and experience, not from someone else. Most people associate creativity with terms like *unique* or *out of the box*. A creative thought can, in this way, resemble or be the same as an inspired moment. But creativity alone does not guarantee functionality and "good."

When you extend a moment's thought, another element of creativity comes into play. That is *assembly*, or how you assemble your inspired thought or thoughts, and convey and apply them to others—this implies expansion, deletion, and organization, as well as the ability to identify "new," perhaps inspired approaches to these components. Remember that winter is the energy of stepping back, looking, and assembling creatively.

Consider this: I can give five people a list of details about an event and ask them to assemble the details into a story. Individuals who have learned their "lessons" well and yet aren't very creative at all can assemble a perfectly procedural story. Other individuals will be perplexed and make a mess of everything. Still others will assemble the overall piece in a way that dazzles the rest of us with its freshness, because few others will have thought of or felt their angle.

There is a wonderful piece of journalism that has become a classic in the field. It is a story titled "Digging JFK's Grave Was His Honor," and it appeared in the *New York Herald Tribune*, Tuesday, November 26, 1963, the day after Kennedy's burial. The piece was written by Pulitzer Prize–winning journalist Jimmy Breslin.

The reason I like this story as an example of creativity is that it is more than just another famous article. It is visionary and iconic. Like Joseph Heller's great *Catch 22*, Breslin's work became so influential that it morphed into a colloquialism and changed the world of news writing. Let me explain. With all of the news coverage of JFK's assassination, and with so many of the dramatic images of that event already locked in people's memories, probably for life, Breslin, as was the rest of media, was faced with the challenge of writing yet another story, this one covering JFK's funeral. How many stories had already been written about the assassination, about Jackie, about the Kennedy family lineage, and so on? How many more would be written about the funeral? With the public already saturated in information, how could a writer make people feel anything new, let alone be interested in his version of an event that would be covered worldwide?

Remember what we said earlier about assembly and creativity. These two factors were the genius that I believe separated Jimmy Breslin's piece from everyone else's.

Standing back and taking a long look at the events preceding the funeral, Breslin took his story down a completely different path than did his colleagues. Breslin chose to write his story from the everyday perspective of a gravedigger, a man by the name of Clifton Pollard. And that "assembly" made all the difference. By telling the story from the perspective of the gravedigger, an ordinary person like the rest of us, Breslin was able to weave "everyman" themes into his story that opened up a whole new window of sensitivities into the Kennedy assassination. There was no Oprah back then, no confessional television where celebrities went national with their feelings. Yet, through Pollard's rendition of events, Breslin was able to capture Jackie as a woman whose husband was murdered next to her, who "had this terrible strength that everybody needed so badly." In the article, Pollard is said to have been unable to attend the funeral himself. He was somewhere else in the cemetery, digging graves for other people, at $3.01 an hour. That was Pollard's job.

Creating the contrast between Pollard and Jackie, and between President Kennedy and the gravesite, shattered conventional reporting structure and drove Breslin's piece in unique directions, making deeply human connections. Among articles that had become run-of-the-mill, Breslin's article was able to rouse compassion not just for Kennedy's death, but also for every human—readers included. It was Breslin's unique assembly of details that placed this story in literary history. Since then, the phrase, "Find the grave digger" has been used as a colloquialism by editors to direct reporters to find that unique angle on a story that will set it apart from all the others that will be written on the same topic that day.

Inspiration

Like Breslin, the creative individual will find the unique assembly of details within her own life—even though, upon first perusal, they may not look unique. She will use winter's pause to bring things side by side (sometimes by additions, other times by deletions) to become fresh and new once assembled as a whole.

Like Breslin, the winter person is not afraid to let go of old habits of the ego, old ways of thinking, and old teachings in order to have his epiphany as well as assemble his dream into a functional whole.

Life is not static. When your creativity flows from your centered Self, it seeds your future with greater potential, less conflict, and more satisfaction.

Entering Your Purest Potential

With your creativity and inspiration heightened, winter is a time for more dreaming and for tapping into your purest potential. For most of us, this season is also a time of holidays, and our lives can become busy with excessive socializing. The challenge is finding and making time to pursue your dreams in quietude.

Take care during the holidays not to reset your social needs—the result of being on one hiatus after another. It's easy to find yourself operating in a *new normal* that can be illusory, leaving you wanting more from daily routines, more than you may usually need. Remember, one of the side effects of those perfect-10 days is that atypical and over-exciting experiences make even better-than-ordinary days seem dull. Then that perception dulls your mood, sending your positive M.O. downward. So our need to socialize will probably be spiked after the exciting holidays.

Nonetheless, make time to be alone. And being alone does not have to mean being lonely—far from it, really. It is the time during which you can best tap this season's energy for discovering your potentials. Flowing across your mental Wi-Fi are constellations of internal and external data you can peruse and combine into an infinite assortment of little packages. Each bundle of information, energized with creativity and your personal thoughts, can be stored and continually updated and reorganized. Many of these bundles of data and energy will evolve into your personal growth.

Set aside some quiet time and space as often as you can. Relax and meditate.

- ෨ **Ask:** What is important to me now?
- ෨ **Pay attention:** Not just to answers, but to incomplete answers, feelings, and even images that may pass through your mind.
- ෨ **Pay attention:** To how further thoughts on the issue and your thoughts and feelings about it emerge throughout the rest of the day.
- ෨ **Action:** Let the contents of your "bundle" keep emerging, redefining, expanding.

Reward yourself at the end of each day for bringing yourself closer to what is important.

The good news is that out of winter's dark, all things become possible. When your bundles of energy and ideas are released into spring, the new you will begin.

How to Optimize Your Winter Energy

The winter cycle is transcendental. Its cool, waning energy nourishes your own tendency toward rest and reflection and deeper moments. This is the energy of creativity in its barest essence. Within this cycle, you can restore yourself and renew your life endlessly. Slow down; take your time to find, assemble, and package your deeper dreams. Store them. Let them soak in potential and re-imagination until the cycles begin again.

Exercises

- **Be silent.** Take some time each day and just sit silently somewhere comfy. Make tea or another warm, relaxing drink. Let your mind be like a still lake, letting pleasant images float across it, letting nothing stick. Just watch objectively and without judgment. You can achieve optimum results if you do this twice a day: once in the morning and again in the evening, for about 20 to 30 minutes each time. Watch and listen without judgment.

- **Dress warm.** But don't overdo it. Feel and appreciate the power of winter. It is good to feel the chill and then return to your warm home or workplace. That feeling is comforting. Try to commit it to memory.

- **Spend some time reading and writing.** Evenings are a good time to nestle up with a warm drink (teas or coffees, even a little wine) and read or write. This is a good combination to do together. Read something that is related to your writing.

- **Get more sleep.** This may mean getting to bed earlier. Sometimes this is difficult because of long habits; however, the payoff is worth it.

- **Make a playlist.** Make a playlist of various natural water sounds. Use these to soothe you whenever you find yourself anxious this season.

- **Be patient.** In order to stay fluid and supple, practice more patience with others and yourself, especially during this season. Put your attention on some of the subtle signs that you are becoming impatient and irritated—particular thoughts, feelings, and actions you are prone to. When you feel these coming on, they are your telltale sign to start compensating, tipping your mental balance back to center. Just as some individuals would compensate for the effects of alcohol coming on—before they do—by being more observant, and moving more slowly and with more precision, you can begin to compensate for thoughts, feelings, and actions you are about to have due to impatience.

- **Try Chi Kung, Tai Chi, or yoga in the snow.** This works great to supercharge you, especially in the early mornings. At night, these activities can have a wonderful calming effect.

- **Power-walk outside.** Try some power-walking, especially in the morning when things are just brightening and all is quiet and still. I find that adding to, varying, or modifying exercise programs within each season keeps the spark high. So if you usually jog five times a week, try jogging four and power-walking one day for something different and special.

- **Hike or rock climb.** Winter hiking is a good way to stay energized and healthy. Try snowshoeing if you are in (or can get to) an area where there is snow. Cross-country skiing is also good winter exercise. These activities are good for bleeding off some of that jumpy energy or anxiety as well as generating some clean, fresh energy to get you going.

- **Massage yourself.** You can self-massage various acupressure points to help spike or even out your energy during this season. Each of these is designed to open up energy blocks in your body. As each opens, you will feel a surge of clean energy that has staying power. I personally do not utilize these more than once a day.

* **Kidney rub.** Sit and relax. Rub your hands together to warm them. Then gently rub the area of your lower back, above the kidneys, in circular motions (just a few passes). You can feel an almost immediate energy release.

* **Bubbling well rub.** This area is located at the bottom of your feet. The "bubbling well" is at the bottom center of your foot. You can get to it from a sitting position and, depending on your balance, from a standing position too (this works great before, after, or during a shower). Locate the area. Start with either foot. Hold your foot with your opposite hand and then gently massage the center area in circular motions with your thumb or thumbs (just a few passes). You can feel an almost immediate energy release. This is a great massage to trade with your partner, family member, or friend.

* **Arm and leg massage.** Use the tips of your right hand fingers to gently tap the right side of your left wrist. Then, follow that "line" straight up to your shoulder. Do the same for your other arm, starting with the left side of the wrist and going up. You can massage your legs the same way, following the same "lines" on each leg.

ᔐ **Stay hydrated.** Remember, the water element is strongest in winter. It is easy to begin working and really forget to drink some water.

ᔐ **Be efficient.** Take the path of least resistance. Water doesn't try to roll over a stone or even a boulder, it just does. It doesn't try to fit into a container, it just does. Ocean tides don't try to rise and fall, they just do. Snow doesn't try to shine in the sunlight or under the stars, it just does. You can, during the winter season, use nature's falling energy to help you become more efficient. Pick a day. Put your attention on how you move physically and mentally from one situation to the next. See where your thoughts and movements are inefficient. Consider ways you can tighten this up. You may consider reflecting on these situations at the end of the day and visualizing yourself activating the behaviors you think will help you be more resourceful. Give yourself a plan to organize daily routines so that you will slow down or so that you can rest between things.

ᔐ **Keep exercising.** But don't overdo it. It is too easy to deplete energy during this season of falling energy. Listen to your body. On some days you will distinctly feel you can do more, but don't push it. Many of us can become compulsive about exercise programs during winter, which makes you want to push when it is not the right time. Avoid that. Try taking on something new as an extra part of your week's workout program instead. So instead of jogging every day, you can do some light weightlifting or yoga or pilates instead or in between days. You may wish to explore the Chinese arts of *Tai Chi* and *Chi Kung* or a Japanese *Karate*. This is a great time of year to begin. The excitement of something new may be just what you need, and you won't have to push it.

ஐ **Let the sun shine.** Try to get as much natural light as you can into your work and living space during daylight hours.

ஐ **Use color.** The holidays are an easy and enjoyable time to add all kinds of color to your living and working space. Uplifting reds and comforting greens work well when you need a lift, and to enhance your inward and waning energies, light and dark blues, combinations of lighter blues and whites, and blacks all work well.

ஐ **Use fragrance.** The holiday season provides wonderful opportunities for using scent to brighten your days and spirit. Refreshing scents such as lotus, cedar, forest, orange, eucalyptus, juniper, and lavender are abundant.

Don't forget about scents attached to many good memories, such as the smell of a natural pine tree, holiday candles, perfumes and colognes, and, of course, your parents' and grandparents' home cooking. These can lighten and brighten your spirit the minute you walk into your home.

ஐ **Stretch.** Be sure to practice a warm-up routine before beginning any exercise. This season, especially, I find it necessary to increase these activities, both before and after workouts. Go slow. Don't overdo it.

ຣ **Spend the day without nitpicking.** Choose a day to try to accurately and objectively observe what is going on without getting judgmental or looking for anything beyond seeing the way things are for you and others. See how you feel at the end of the day.

ຣ **Flow.** Identify various activities that already work for you to get your mind flowing. Apply these in the morning to get you started, around midday, and whenever else you need it to keep you flowing throughout the day. Holiday playlists work great. You can combine these with video and/or photo slide shows for an even stronger effect. Being prepared in advance is worth its weight in gold when you are experiencing one of those low-energy mornings or afternoons.

ຣ **Meditate.** When you enter the cold, find the warmth inside yourself. Try to see it spreading throughout your body. Then later, try it in a meditation. Let your mind identify where you are feeling cold externally, and let it gravitate to a place of warmth inside yourself. Take a slow, deep breath. Use your breath to guide the warmth inside you to where you are feeling cold, and vice versa. Practice this movement often until you ingrain it in your mind. Then use this movement to change your disposition the next time you are in a situation in which you feel yourself inappropriately fired up; becoming irritated, anxious, or fearful about something; or feeling inappropriately detached from something.

ຣ **Practice Xin-Yi (heart-mind).** In Chinese the term *Xin-Yi* means "heart-mind." It is a core concept in holistic arts and consciousness training. Believed by the ancients to be enormously empowering, Xin-Yi is a coveted mindset.

In order to activate Xin-Yi, first relax and place your mind in a meditative mindset. Then, use your mind to feel the coolness of winter on your skin, then the warmth below that, then the coolness below that. Now, put your attention on your heart's desires (*Xin*), not what other factors in your environment desire for you. This may be an image, a feeling, a thought or narrative, and so on. Let it float through your mind. Just observe it. Then put your attention on your reasoning (*Yi*) or intentional skills and see (again, letting things float through) how your desire fits in with other images, feelings, and thoughts you have had—especially throughout the year thus far, but not restricted only to these. Consider various creative ways you could "assemble" these. If necessary, sketch out some possible drafts later so you can remember different variations. Keep your bundles of information alive in your mind by revisiting them often to add, expand, and delete information. Some individuals don't reactivate these often enough and so there is not much energy within. This can be a mistake. You want to energize these to the point of making them reflexive in your mind. This way, when you release them into spring, as opportunities arise, they will activate automatically and assist you in achieving your dreams.

ॐ **Nurture your creativity.** Go to a lecture; read something new and different; go to a play or musical or movie that you believe can inspire new ideas on how you can more creatively scaffold one of your dreams.

∞ **Eat warmer and more nourishing foods.** These can include soups, stews, root vegetables, whole grains, barley, beans, fish, eggs, meats (pork, lamb) in moderation, and nuts. Pears and other naturally sweeter fruits are especially healthy for you during this season. Bear in mind, you can also cook your pears to add more moisture. Take care not to overeat. Try some dark chocolate. Dark, leafy vegetables and fish (salmon) are especially good this time of year.

How to Correct Winter Imbalances

Shannon is a single mom of three children, ages 3 to 9. She currently works in research and development for a high-tech company, and enjoys her work. Her background is in electrical engineering. As well as being interested in scientific study, she also enjoys art—she has ever since her first art class in high school. She even considered art as a major when she went to college, but decided on engineering instead.

A few years ago, a friend of hers, who also has three children, showed her a winter holiday decoration she had made with her kids. It was of three almost-life-sized, two-dimensional, painted plywood figures (caricatures) of the children. Her friend displayed them side by side on her front porch.

Shannon loved the idea and thought to try making a set with her own kids. So she priced the wood she would need for construction. She also shopped online for other outdoor decorations, something seasonal and with lights. Somewhere between looking at other decorations with lights and getting ready to purchase the wood to make her plywood figures, Shannon had an idea. She thought, instead of pursuing the wooden figures, to combine her art and electrical skills. She took her idea to the drawing board and designed a wooden star that was 6 feet in height and could be made from the plywood she was planning on purchasing. She also designed a layout of lights that would be attached to the piece so that it would be fully illuminated. Then, she and her children made a project of purchasing the necessary materials and building their holiday star. They attached it to their home so that, at night, it could be seen brightly glowing, even from far away. Constructing their project became a winter event for the family and brought them all a deep sense of pleasure and peace. It created a memory they would all draw positive energy from in the days ahead.

ভ

Ted dug into his creative reserves and was inspired to transform several rooms in his home to get his mind flowing with positivity during the winter. He felt he reaped double rewards: a nicer living space and a healthier, happier mindset.

Ted worked alone. His idea originated as a spinoff from restoring a piece of old furniture he had gotten the summer before (which had been sitting in his garage for a few months). The piece was an old dresser he had found marked "Free" on someone's front lawn. Ted noticed that working with his hands (as opposed to the deskwork he does daily) felt great. It calmed him down, which he needed, and got him out of his head. After the dresser, he went on to painting his foyer a brighter color so that when he arrived home in the evenings he would be receive a boost of cheer and a good memory to re-charge him. He then moved on to decorating for the holidays, rearranging furniture in several rooms of the house and even rearranging materials on the many bookshelves. This all kept his mind flowing, which translated to smoother workdays and even better sleep.

The holistic arts maintain that the winter cycle embodies the restorative and creative power you need to rebound, reinvent, and rebuild yourself. The process is natural and synergistic: After you extend energy, you must pause and recharge before you can reach out again. When you rebuild, you must pause to take a look at what's been going on, what is going on, and where you want to be headed. You are doing more than simply adding another detail onto a string of details. As both Shannon and Ted learned, winter energy is about weaving together and harmonizing your past, present, and future so that what comes up next connects for you in a more deeply satisfying way and continues to grow from who you are, not from what or where someone else thinks you should be.

So there is some toggling going on during this season between the energies from other seasons and the winter cycle because you will need, when necessary, spring's quick bursts of energy to jumpstart you; summer's fire to bring you to various finish lines; autumn's boundaries and pruning to eliminate the unreasonable and nurture healthy, authentic growth; and especially late summer's core energy, your CEO of Self, to help you manage it all with purpose.

Winter is the season of water, deep restoration, and purification. It helps you step back, locate your center, deepen your Self-awareness, and identify and assemble new bundles of possibilities that you will seed in the spring.

Let's take a closer look at some common imbalances associated with the winter cycle and at how winter's natural energy can help you reverse these tendencies and bring you back to a state of balance.

During winter, the mind and body continue to be under the influence of nature's falling energy. Even though this is a time of great restoration and creativity, imbalances during this season can leave you feeling fatigued and "down in the dumps" rather than imaginative and purposeful. Anxieties, as could have become the case for both Shannon and Ted, can arise from lacking the physical and psychic energy needed to get your usual jobs done and to keep the mind in a state of flow. These anxieties can affect your coping mechanisms and result in emotional swings and depression. As days get colder, as light gets sparser, and as life demands keep pouring on, imbalances may result in over-exertion. Yet, many still try to keep the pace, rather than change it to synchronize with nature's falling energy. Behavior can become lackadaisical and detached or swing the other way and become harmfully aggressive. Imbalance can further manifest in poor reasoning, loss of memory, and joint and muscle pain.

Yet the winter cycle offers you the cooler, slower energy you will need to stabilize. The following is a list of activities to help you tap in.

- **Correct low energy.** Whenever you want to increase your energy, calm yourself first. Psychologically and physically, any benefits you receive from activity intended to energize you will be more amplified if you first proceed from a calmed mindset. Then, if you are lacking reserves, and feeling depleted motivation or physical strength, try asking yourself a few questions.

  * **Ask:** Why do I feel my energy is low? Am I pushing too hard in any one direction? Are my energies too divided—am I spread too thin? Are my feelings depleting my energy? Am I getting more sleep than I did last cycle? Am I eating nutritiously?

  * **Ask:** How have I dealt with similar issues when I am on top of my game?

  * **Ask:** Do I want to change anything about the way I am dealing with issues now?

✳ **Take charge:** Remember, our bodies are vessels and they can only hold a certain amount of energy. The idea is to release the bad and replenish with good. Generally, you can begin by calming yourself down, using any of the relaxing techniques in this book or any others that work for you. Then apply any of the energy-building activities we've covered. This will help you gain more energy, and once you can maintain your balance even a little, your process becomes its own reward: You will feel better even before you engage in your "feel better" activity because you are anticipating its results. Psychologically, expectation and reward is great this way. You will notice you start feeling better the next time you apply your personal prescription as soon as you begin, merely in the anticipation of feeling better. In this way, you are training your mind to trust itself. You are using intrinsic reward to make yourself feel good—to enter and sustain a state of flow. Doing this can snowball the whole process: You're feeling good, you are expecting to feel even better, you feel rewarded, your energy goes up, and your mind becomes positive and energized again. You are using your mind-body "currency" to get you flowing and keep you there.

❦ **Reverse excessive energy.** Sometimes during the winter cycle it is easy to feel that your energy is mismatched because you are anxious or jumpy. The contrast in the environment around you only makes this imbalance feel more pronounced. One way you can deal with this is to create an internal leveling tool. Many occupations use some kind of leveling tool to indicate irregularities and imbalances. Today, most of these instruments are laser-driven. However, you may have seen some of the older models with a glass portal filled with fluid and an air bubble that moved side to side and eventually rested in the center when everything was lined up or balanced. Here is how you can create an internal leveling tool to help yourself reach balance when you need to.

∗ Everybody tends to get used to breathing shallow. Next thing you know, shallow breathing begins to feel normal and becomes your habit (or new normal). Try breathing big—taking exaggerated, deep in-breaths through your nose that go all the way to the bottom of your feet. Then let out a long exhale through your mouth. Do this a few times—as long as you are comfortable doing so. Then, reset your breathing to a depth and rhythm that feels more balanced.

∗ If you are feeling jumpy with excessive mismatched energy, go to the extreme opposite. This will make the contrast big. When you go big, it will make the point of "center" or balance more apparent. So slow down your actions and thinking to an extreme and look for your happy medium.

∗ Actively do nothing. Another version of "going big" when your energy is excessive is to take a whole day off and actively do nothing. This doesn't mean computing, talking on the phone, watching television, reading, or doing chores. Do absolutely nothing. This will restore your energy and help you reset your internal compass to a place of balance.

✳ If you are compulsive about something, for example, spending, go big in the opposite direction. Spend nothing at all, except for bare necessities, for one pay period. This will help you better locate the balance between spending that is frivolous and spending that is necessary.

❧ **Reverse fear.** We are more prone to fear during the winter cycle. Part of the reason is that our energy slips out of sync with the falling energy of the season. Another reason is that we get used to old habits and routines that worked once, particularly during those high-gear activities of summer, and are not working so well now that nature's energy is falling. It's easy to suddenly find yourself scrambling to fit the pieces of your life together and fearing the consequences of not being able to. You have to modify and adjust, but that can be difficult. Change triggers a lot of emotions—among them, fear. Fear then creates anxiety, makes us feel ungrounded, and can paralyze performance.

Although fear can be healthy, especially when it keeps us from harm, it is often rough on you. Here are a few tips for reversing it once it becomes unhealthy.

First, find that "cool," wintery place inside yourself and summon it to siphon away your anxiety and literally chill you out. Revitalize yourself with this winter mix. It's okay to overcompensate a little, indulging in it until you are cooled down enough to feel and think more objectively.

Then, find your center from there, using the energy you felt in summer's heat to get you there. Feel that safe warmth in your heart, giving you strength and protecting you. Once calm, let a feeling of love and summer power flow through you. Then, from that optimized mindset:

* Identify that you are fearful.

* Identify whether the subject of your fear is a real threat or a non-threat you perceive as a threat. **Ask:** Are there any indications that this is less of a threat than I am feeling? How do others perceive this?

* How have I perceived similar situations before? What was the outcome then? Did my response bring me closer to or further from what I needed?

* Be flexible.

* Do I want to change anything about my former response?

* If you are dealing with a non-threat, dismiss it.

* If you are dealing with a genuine threat, **ask:** What qualities of water suggest the right movement, softness, solidity, invisibility, speed, stillness? What tools will I need to deal with the threat? Patience? Verbal skill? Empathy?

Objectivity? Historical perspective? Technical perspective?

✳ Imagine a person you know who has these qualities. How would that person navigate through the situation?

✳ **Ask:** Which tools do I already have? How can I acquire those I do not possess?

℘ **Reverse depression.** Winter's falling energy makes some individuals feel down and out. You may feel like getting out of your own head, and perhaps even doing something destructive to get you there—like drinking or drugging or the like. What you may need instead is to get more objectively *into* your own mind. Because you are feeling seasonal blahs you may begin to lose your motivation and withdraw until you start feeling swept away by your feelings, and they spiral down into depression.

One possible reason for this trek is that as nature's energy continues to slow down, many of us just keep barreling forward as if nothing has changed. Some feel they cannot keep up with life's demands. Some feel they cannot keep up with routines. Expectations reverse from the anticipation of reward to anticipating losing reward. Just as reward can create a loop of positive energy, its opposite can push us into a downward cycle.

✳ Embrace the slower pace initiated by nature.

✳ Spend some time each evening (or over the weekend) identifying ways you can meet your daily challenges more efficiently so that you can fall into a naturally slower pattern. Implement these.

* Use exercise to stimulate your energy and uplift your spirit. Outdoor activity is especially good.

* Spend some time each day dreaming of your future possibilities. Put your focus on assets—people, places, things, and so on—you have accrued in the past year (and even prior) and on a variety of ways you can creatively "assemble" these details into your future dreams. All you are doing is window shopping in your mind. So give yourself the freedom to assemble without restriction. Store these in your mental shopping cart and move on to more possibilities. Revisit each and add whenever you can.

* Get more and *better* sleep. For optimal sleep, try using your "insomnia" playlist before getting your Zs. Combine your playlist with a meditation and/or visualization. Use nightly and whenever you awaken during the night.

ℂ **Reverse dysfunctional cravings.** Again, watch out for dysfunctional cravings associated with energy loss, such as for carbohydrates and caffeine. The crash that goes along with these isn't always worth the momentary pick-me-up. Moderation is key. Use meditation and exercise instead. A few good workouts throughout the week can help energize you, strengthen your motivation, and get you back on track. They will give your mind and body a hormonal cocktail to help lift your mood as well as improve your focus and memory.

ৰ **Reverse poor decision-making.** Choose a day and make a list of all the decisions you make (that day) that you consider made with poor judgment.

* **Ask:** Why did I choose as I did?

* **Ask:** What was going on that made me choose this way?

* **Ask:** How did my choices make me feel, emotionally and physically?

* **Ask:** How did my choices and feelings affect other factors in my day?

* The next day, when confronted with decisions, step back, remember the effect of winter's chill on your focus—slow down, sharpen your concentration, and lose the heat of negative emotions. Then, take a look at your options. Choose what is best for your interests and most appropriate to the situation.

ৰ **Reverse insomnia.** Some people have difficulty falling asleep; others wake up earlier than necessary; and still others wake up on and off throughout the night. Insomnia can result from an inability to resolve a conflict, adding to anxiety and emotional distress and becoming a potentially destructive cycle.

* **Ask:** What is distressing me, and why? Your stress may be coming from disorganization or a need to slow your pace. It may be coming from feeling that you don't have the energy to meet

important daily responsibilities in your personal life. You may need to begin to explore new dreams and directions. It may be coming from fear.

* **Action:** Give yourself a time limit to think about it, then a better time (*times* if you need more than one) when you can return to the issue the next day or later.

* **Action:** Create a calming musical playlist to re-set. Use this playlist only for this purpose.

* **Action:** Avoid caffeinated drinks, especially af-ter dinner, and decrease your intake during the day.

* **Action:** Identify household problems with distraction—for example, late-night television, noise, and so on. Try to manage these.

∞ **Give something back to the world.** Use your skills to help someone else through an imbalance this sea-son. This is the best way not only to sharpen your own techniques but also to learn new skills. You will also be recycling your own and nature's energy and emptying your cup so that you are ready for more goodness. And so the cycle continues.

How to Cultivate the Spirit of Winter

A Winter Meditation

All that we have seen in nature is a macrocosm of what goes on in the mind and body. There is no boundary.

This is because we are part of nature and nature is part of us. So if you want to know what goes on in the mind and body, look into the environment where the message is scaled so big that it is easier to see.

Nature teaches us to find our own deeper stillness during winter. Within this quietude, we can fulfill our need for a deeper sense of calm. This is the energy required to generate fresh, new creative directions in our lives—big or small. Here you will find guidance, efficiency, and restoration throughout the coming months and whenever else you need.

Take some time for yourself each day (or night) to just get out and be still with nature. Use the winter coolness to shut off your thoughts and send your attention to the present. Fill your focus with wintery images that have a positive effect on you.

Once your mind's visual files are wide open, slow and measure your breathing. Relax. Take a slow look around the landscape (physically in your environment or within your mind).

Identify the natural stillness in things; the pocket of white light filling random spaces carved out of snow, there one minute, gone the next. The stripes of blue-grey light that dip across an open field; the low gurgling of moving water. Let these images float across your mind. Observe them. Do not disturb them. Just watch them. Look closely and with patience at any one object. Try to see the subtle changes that occur from one moment to the next. This takes patience, but you will see: the one brown leaf that moments ago was still as a brush stroke on a painting, suddenly stirs—then others, then all seems still again, but not—not really. All is in constant flux, just slowly, slowly evolving, flowing, into the next moment. Let nature speak its message to you. Find peace in her. Let her guide you to the peace in you.

Look for the intelligence of winter. See the new tree in its first winter or the old tree or the bird or chipmunk, the snow slowly piling on a mailbox.

Even big change is sometimes subtle until you freeze it and look closely—and examine. When we have too many programs open in our mind, even big change is sometimes hard to see. But be assured it is happening.

How does the sky look different this time of year? Consider a pond or a lake. How does it appear different?

What of the creatures? Visualize all those who are hibernating—ants, ladybugs, snakes, and butterflies burrowing under the tree bark, and bears. Visualize the fish alive below the ice; see eggs and microorganisms. Visualize the birds who have migrated, and those who have not.

Think of all the new and good elements that have entered your life in the past year. Perhaps they are playing underneath the more obvious programs running in your mind. But once you relax, once you "cool down," you can see them. In the hustle and bustle of our lives, the tiniest, subtlest aspects of our inner landscape can go unseen. But once you slow down and patiently look, they are there within the cycle. Have patience.

Ask yourself: *If I could create my innermost dream, what would it look like?* Be creative. Be free to think "outside the box." Try to see this. Slow your breathing. Take a deep breath. Exhale slowly. Take a close look. Grow this dream.

Resolutions

Winter

- ❧ Today I will befriend winter's energy within me.

- ❧ Today I will remember to slow down.

- ❧ Today I will make time to be out of doors.

- ❧ Today I will spend some quiet time considering where I have been, where I am at the moment, and where I dream to be in the future.

- ❧ Today I will think of ways I could reasonably accomplish my dreams, even if in small steps.

- ❧ Today I will help someone else accomplish his or her vision.

- ❧ Today I will practice patience.

- ❧ Today I will give myself extra time to get to where I am going.

- ❧ Today I will organize so that I will not spread myself too thin.

- ❧ Today I will actively remember that I am free to choose my reactions to challenges.

- ❧ Today I will look for opportunities to dismiss non-threatening situations.

- ❧ Today I will not defend my thinking on things. I will listen to others' thoughts and not get stuck to any. I will practice observing and hearing.

- ❧ Today I will be like water.

ॐ Today I will look for an opportunity to give something back to the Universe. I will use my creativity and an element of my Self to create something that can help someone else.

> *From point comes a line, then a circle;*
> *When the circle is complete,*
> *Then the last is joined to the first.*
> —Shabistari

GLOSSARY

assembly: how you organize your inspired thoughts to convey and apply them to others

center of balance: midpoint or core

center: midpoint, point of balance, or core

CEO: chief executive officer

chakra system: energy centers within the body, where energy enters the body, is processed, and is sent out again

chi: life-force energy, power, spirit, or energy flowing within and through all things

chi kung: a Chinese holistic art that focuses on harnessing chi for the purpose of health as well as physical and emotional strength

cognitive: involving cognition or the processes of knowing through perception, learning, and reasoning

C-suite: executive suite

Dan Tien: the body's energy center, a few inches above the navel

disassociation: having one's emotions detached

down energy: falling energy; calming

ego: what you think you want, what you will to believe, what you think you can afford, what you decide to love, what you regard yourself bound to

emotional swings: mood swings; ups and downs

energetically systemic: throughout the entire system

flow: a state of concentration so focused that it amounts to absolute absorption in an activity

flowing: a state of flow

heart chakra: the body's energy center associated with the heart

hub: center, root

Indian summer: an unseasonably warm and sunny patch of weather during autumn

Karate: a martial art developed on Okinawa, from Chinese kenpo and kung fu

Law of Attraction: like attracts like, as in positivity attracts positivity

middle country: China

middle: center

midlife crisis: a "crisis" occurring in a person's middle years that involves a disconnect between what the individual has become and the person he or she is internally

Mushin: Japanese for "empty mind"

non-centered mind: imbalanced

perceive: the act of perception

perception: the conscious acknowledgement and interpretation of sensory stimuli

psychological currency: good for the mind; psychic energy

pure awareness: that part of your mind that is self-aware

reference point: a person who has successfully navigated through a similar situation

rising and falling energy: waxing and waning energy arcs and cycles

rising energy: waxing

root: center

Self: who you are and what you are feeling on the inside

sensei: martial arts teacher, in Japanese; the word means "to give birth"

Tai Chi: often spelled *taiji*; a martial art that originated in the Shaolin temple of China and is characterized by deep explorations of chi

TCM: Traditional Chinese Medicine

top-down processing: information processing based on previous knowledge, expectations, and plans of action

Traditional Chinese Medicine: a system of medicine based on whole-person health and healing, emphasizing balance, synchronicity, and prevention of problems before they occur

universal consciousness: God

universal movements: seasons, cycles

up energy: rising energy

vernal equinox: begins spring March 20

xin: heart's desire

Xin-Yi: heart-mind

INDEX

ABOUT THE AUTHOR

Joseph Cardillo, PhD, is a top-selling author in the fields of health, mind-body-spirit, and psychology. He is an expert in **Attention Training**™ and creative thinking. Dr. Cardillo has taught his methods to more than 20,000 students in various colleges, universities, and institutes. His books—*The Five Seasons: Tap Into Nature's Secrets for Health, Happiness, and Harmony*; *Can I Have Your Attention? How to Think Fast, Find Your Focus, and Sharpen Your Concentration*; *Your Playlist Can Change Your Life*; *Be Like Water*; and *Bow to Life*—have inspired people of all ages worldwide. Foreign language editions of his work have appeared in German, Russian, Portuguese, Arabic, Korean, Malaysian, Chinese,

Turkish, Spanish, and Hindi. A regular contributor to the *Huffington Post* and *Psychology Today*, he holds a doctorate in holistic psychology and mind-body medicine, and is a research associate at Mind-Body Medical University. In 2011 Dr. Cardillo received the prestigious *SUNY Chancellor's Award for Scholarly Research and Creative Activity*.

In addition, he co-writes books for Harvard Health Publications.

Feature articles on Dr. Cardillo's work have appeared in *Smithsonian Magazine*, *The New York Post*, *The Los Angeles Times*, *The Toronto Globe*, *Men's Health*, *Men's Fitness*, *Family Circle*, *FIRST for Women*, *Curve*, *American Fitness Magazine*, *Fitness Magazine*, *Natural Health*, *Natural Solutions*, and *GoodHouseKeeping.com*. He was interviewed, based on his book *Be Like Water*, for the documentary film *Looking for Mr. Miyagi*, scheduled for a 2013 release.

Specialties: Attention Training™, mind-body health, creative thinking.

Website: *www.josephcardillo.com*